CU00922199

Double-Crossing the Gold Dust Trio: Stanislaus Zbyszko's Last Hurrah

By Ken Zimmerman Jr.

Double-Crossing the Gold Dust Trio: Stanislaus Zbyszko's Last Hurrah

Published in St. Louis, Missouri by Ken Zimmerman Jr. Enterprises.

First Edition: August 2021

If you like this book, you can sign up for Ken's newsletter to receive information about future book releases. You can sign up for the newsletter and receive a free e-book at kenzimmermanjr.com.

Dedication

I am dedicating this book to Stanislaus Zbyszko, a criminally underrated world class wrestler.

Figure 1- Stanislaus Zbyszko on the left around the time he wrestled "Big" Wayne Munn (Public Domain)

Table of Contents

Introduction

For five years in the mid-1920s, the Gold Dust Trio of promoter Billy Sandow, World Heavyweight Wrestling Champion Ed "Strangler" Lewis and booking genius Joe "Toots" Mondt dominated American professional wrestling. With a stranglehold on the World Title, no pun intended, they wrung concessions from promoters wanting to book the World Champion. "Toots" Mondt changed the style of wrestling to a more action-packed match.

Wilhelm Baumann, better known as Billy Sandow, was born in Rochester, New York on September 4, 1884. Sandow began physical culture training, an early version of bodybuilding, as a teenager. Developing a powerful physique, Baumann began wrestling at the beginning of the 20th Century.

Legend has it that Wilhelm Baumann was a huge fan of 19th Century physical culturist, and sometimes wrestler, Eugene Sandow. When Baumann began wrestling, he adopted the name "Billy Sandow" as a tribute to his hero.

Sandow's biggest weakness in the ring was his size. Although powerful, he normally weighed between 155 and 165 pounds.

Sandow's brother Max Baumann, who wrestled under his real name, travelled with his brother both wrestling and later promoting events. Max Baumann would be a key player in the event, which led to the downfall of the Gold Dust Trio.

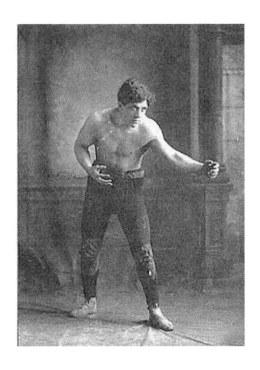

Figure 2-Billy Sandow as a young wrestler (Public Domain)

As Sandow moved more into management and promotion, he realized that a few promoters like Jack Curley of New York exercised significant influence because of their control of both a huge market and a cozy relationship with the governing bodies like the New York State Athletic Commission.

To counteract this influence and build his own circuit in case of conflicts, Curley was notoriously difficult to have a good relationship with, Sandow convinced several men to move to Midwestern cities to setup wrestling promotions. Sandow helped the men by providing stars like Lewis for their shows.

Sandow chose the Midwest because of a strong fan base for wrestling as well as larger cities like St. Louis, Kansas City, Missouri, and Omaha. While many of these cities had promotions starting up, Wichita, with a population of 72,000, didn't have a local promoter.

Sandow convinced Tom Law, a barber from Macon, Georgia, who dabbled in promoting wrestling, to relocate to Wichita. Sandow helped Law get his promotion established and provided frequent stars for his cards. Sandow even booked a World Title switch for Wichita in 1922. The Wichita promotion was quite successful until it merged into the Central States promotion in 1959.[i]

Sandow's real claim to fame though was as the manager of Ed "Strangler" Lewis. Lewis would dominate American professional wrestling from the late 1910s to the early 1930s.

Ed "Strangler" Lewis was born Robert Herman Julius Friedrich on June 30, 1891, in Nekoosa, Wisconsin. Lewis participated in many sports but focused strictly on wrestling in his early teens. Lewis already knew he wanted to be a professional wrestler.

Making his professional debut at the unusually young age of 14 years old in Louisville, Kentucky,[ii] he took the name Ed "Strangler" Lewis as an homage to Evan "Strangler" Lewis. Evan Lewis was the greatest professional wrestler from Wisconsin at that time. Evan Lewis was an American Heavyweight Wrestling Champion and one of the meanest wrestlers of all-time. Ed Lewis would one day surpass his namesake as historians consider Ed Lewis or Frank Gotch the greatest American professional wrestler.

In 1905, Lewis was just a young wrestler learning his craft. He wouldn't start to hit his prime until 1915, when he beat most of the competitors in the 1915 International Wrestling Tournament in New York. He only lost one bout in the tournament to Alex Aberg although match was in Aberg's preferred style of Greco-Roman wrestling. Aberg refused to meet Lewis in a catch-as-catch-can bout. I cover this tournament extensively in *Masked Marvel to the Rescue*, one of my previous books.

Lewis was the perfect man to hold the World Championship during the worked era of the 1920s. Lewis could drop his championship to a contender, when Lewis started to get stale, or the Gold Dust Trio wanted to build a new wrestler.

If the wrestler didn't want to drop the title back to Lewis, no problem. Lewis would just take it from the man in a legitimate contest. Since Lewis could wrestle and apply submissions, wrestling Lewis in a legitimate contest came with a high risk of serious injury. Consequently, most wrestlers never entertained the thought of wrestling "the Strangler."

Ed "Strangler" Lewis was already World Champion, when Joe "Toots" Mondt joined the promotional group in 1923. Recommended as a training partner for Lewis by superstar trainer Martin "Farmer" Burns, Mondt quickly proved his value to both Sandow and Lewis.

Joseph Raymond Mondt was born in Gordon Grove, Iowa on January 18, 1894. Like many Iowans, Mondt took to wrestling like a duck to water. Mondt didn't remain in Iowa though as his family moved to Colorado in his young teens.

Mondt made his professional debut in Colorado wrestling all-comers in carnival matches. Carnival matches were "shoots" or legitimate contest, normally with untrained farmers or local athletes selected from the carnival crowd.

The carnival owner would attract the locals by offering a large monetary prize, if the local could last a certain amount of time with the wrestler. Each contestant put up an entry fee to have a chance with the wrestler, who was always a skilled submission wrestler.

Losing one of these matches led to quick unemployment, so Mondt became a talented "hooker" or wrestler skilled in submission moves. Mondt, or the other carnival wrestlers, would "hook" or catch the challenger in a submission. The challenger either submitted or the pro seriously injured them.

This early carnival training helped Mondt hold his own with Lewis in their training sessions. Lewis told Lou Thesz only Mondt and Stanislaus Zbyszko could give him trouble in a legitimate wrestling match.[iii] Lewis' training sessions with Mondt were tougher than 99 percent of his matches.

Mondt's greatest contribution to the team was his innovations in the style of wrestling. The mat wrestling of the day turned off fans. Contests could take hours to determine a winner with little action for extended periods.

My grandfather Gilbert Ellis did not like professional wrestling because he went to the matches with his Uncle Jules Johannpeter at the St. Louis Coliseum in the early 1920s. Grandpa told me that sometimes they would take the streetcar down to the St. Louis Coliseum without eating dinner because of start time for the matches.

He and Uncle Jules would wait for the wrestlers to grab a hold on the mat and Uncle Jules would say, "Let's go." They went across the street to the sandwich shop, ate a sandwich and went back to their seats in the Coliseum. Grandpa told me that most of the time the wrestlers were still in the same position.

Mondt suggested time limits, angles to promote matches and more spectacular moves. Lou Thesz felt Mondt's greatest contribution was the package show. Promoters would hire a group of wrestlers for tours. They would then match those wrestlers against each other in shows across the country.

If a local promoter had some wrestlers, the Gold Dust Trio would work them into the card. Often, a local wrestler would be in the main event against the world champion.

In the match underneath the main event, the Gold Dust Trio would normally build up a challenger for the champion's next title defenses.

The card would normally be three to four matches. On a four-match card, the preliminary bout would be to start building a rookie, the Gold Dust Trio was high on, by giving him a win against a capable but not world champion.

The second match wouldn't have much significance. It could be the promoter's local wrestlers or a couple of Trio managed mid-card wrestlers.

The package show would be the preliminary match, second match (optional), co-main event with a future title challenger and the main event, often for the world championship. Martin "Farmer" Burns did similar things with his group of wrestlers but not according to Mondt's formula nor with Mondt's sped-up style of wrestling.

Mondt also didn't expect the main event to be the only draw for the crowd. He expected the preliminary bout and co-main event build match would also draw fans.

Thesz credited Mondt with revolutionizing professional wrestling, which was extremely high praise. Thesz personally detested Mondt.[iv]

With the promotional skill of Billy Sandow, the innovative and exciting wrestling booked by Mondt and the unquestioned skill of Lewis, the Gold Dust Trio was able to both revolutionize and dominate American professional wrestling in the 1920s. They made so much money that Ed "Strangler" Lewis was the highest paid athlete of the 1920s. While they collaborated with other promoters,

their dominance also made them many
enemies. Those enemies would bide their
time until they could extract their
revenge on the Gold Dust Trio.

Figure 3- Ed "Strangler" Lewis training in 1916 (Public Domain)

Chapter 1 – Lewis vs. Stecher

Before there was the "Gold Dust Trio," it was the Gold Dust Duo of Billy Sandow and Ed "Strangler" Lewis. To realize their plans for American professional wrestling, Sandow first had to secure a World Title match for Lewis. Sandow achieved his goal on Monday, December 13, 1920. Lewis wrestled his greatest rival and business enemy, Joe Stecher. Stecher and Lewis would be in each other's way for most of their careers.

A year before this match, Stecher and Lewis met in a match lasting over three hours. Lewis made a mental error in rushing for Stecher, who was reeling from one of Lewis' headlocks. Lewis tried to pounce on him, but Stecher caught Lewis off-guard throwing him for a fall.

Lewis trained for over a year focused on preventing Stecher surprising him again or losing due to fatigue. Lewis spent the year grinding his headlock on his wooden dummy head fitted with steel springs between the head pieces. He originally used a front face choke, or guillotine choke in Brazilian Jiu-Jitsu, but athletic commissions outlawed the move in the 1910s.

While promoters prearranged mat finishes at the time, Lewis and Stecher legitimately detested each other. According to Lou Thesz, Stecher and Lewis wrestled each other three times over eleven hours before Lewis was finally able to defeat Stecher legitimately.[v]

"My Headlock Will Finish Roller," Says the Strangler

Strangler Lewis' Famous Dummy On Which He Practises the Headlock

A packed house seems assured as the news has gone out to all nearby towns that the big match is to be staged here to-night and all lovers of clean sport and a great fight are coming from miles around to see the two great wrestlers battle for not only the American title but for the honor of a match with Wladek Zbyszko, the Pole, who now holds the world's title.

The struggle itself promises to be one of the grueling nature, of powerful holds, of thrilling and almost superhuman efforts to break the same, and all in all as sensational an affair as was ever staged on the mat in this country.

Ed. (Strangler) Lewis is already in this city waiting for the big match to go on. When told of Roller's unique headlock hold and would break clear of it as did Zbyszko, Lewis issued a statement:

"My headlock is as certain to work to-night against Roller as it ever did. I expect to win in two straight falls and to end all of this talk by the doctor that he will defeat me and then win the world's title from Zbyszko, thus bringing it

ED. "STRANGLER" LEWIS

Figure 4- Strangler Lewis' Spring-Loaded Dummy Head from the Harrisburg, Pennsylvania Newspaper in 1919 (Public Domain)

Lewis always claimed he took the title from Stecher in a "shoot" or legitimate contest, but did he?

21

The match in question occurred in New York's 71st Regiment Armory, a frequent arena for wrestling in New York at the time. 8,000 fans crowded into the armory to see the hated rivals battle over the title.[vi]

Lewis, the challenger, entered the ring wearing a royal purple robe. Frank Gotch also wore a royal purple robe during his title reign causing some reporters to remark that Lewis was trying to establish himself as another Frank Gotch.[vii] Lewis though would achieve greatness in his own right.

Figure 5-Joe Stecher with his championship belt circa 1915 (Public Domain)

Stecher entered the ring next wearing a plain plaid robe along with his championship belt. Lewis was an inch shorter than Stecher but at least thirty pounds heavier. Lewis official weight was

228 but he weighed around 240 pounds. Stecher was a trim 208 pounds at 5'11" tall.

Some unexpected drama, for the fans, occurred before the match as the returning Stanislaus Zbyszko entered the ring to challenger the winner of the match. Zbyszko had been in Europe since 1914. Caught up in World War I, Zbyszko was finally able to return to the United States after several years applying for reentry.

While shaking hands with Stecher, Zbyszko made a playful grab for the champion. However, Stecher resented the playfulness before the match and shoved Zbyszko away.[viii] Zbyszko left the ring muttering curses in Polish.

Joe Stecher was high strung at the best of times. Horse play before a big match was not a distraction he would suffer gladly.

Stecher's stated plan for the match was to counter Lewis' powerful headlock with his leg scissors. To prove the power of his leg scissors hold, Stecher squeezed a bag of hay or animal feed with the leg scissors. Spectators would be shocked when the bags burst due to the squeeze of Stecher's scissors hold.

The men met in the center of the ring for the customary handshake. Lewis was deadly serious, while Stecher wore his normal confident grin although his interaction with Zbyszko betrayed his nervousness. The men shook hands and returned to their corner as referee George Bothner prepared to start the match.

Bothner was the former lightweight wrestling champion. He was also the regular referee chosen by the New York State Athletic Commission to referee matches in New York City. Bothner started the match at 9:20 p.m.

Figure 6- George Bothner in 1908 (Public Domain)

After about 5 minutes of cautious circling, Stecher tried an ankle pick on Lewis, who stepped back away from Stecher's grasp. Lewis countered by leaping for the headlock but missed. Stecher applied a reverse arm lock, but Lewis reversed it on the way to the mat. Stecher ended up on the bottom, where he was stuck for about 10 minutes before escaping and scurrying back to his feet.

Lewis recovered by securing both Stecher's knees together and bringing him back to the mat. Stecher quickly escaped and started back to his feet. Lewis secured the headlock for less than a second before Stecher wriggled free.[ix]

After about 15 minutes, another impediment presented itself to wrestlers, referee, and spectators. Prior to the late 1980s, public smoking in buildings was legal everywhere.

After 15 minutes of the main event, spectators were having trouble seeing the action in the ring from all the smoke in the arena. With that much smoke, breathing must have been difficult for the contestants and referee.[x] Fans saw George Bothner choking and weeping from the thick smoke.

Stecher almost ended the match a few minutes later after securing an arm and body hold on Lewis. He slowly worked Lewis to the ground. One shoulder touched the mat and it looked bad for Lewis.[xi] Lewis, however, worked his bigger body onto his side and squirmed out from underneath Stecher.

As Lewis was trying to get to his feet, Stecher finally had a chance at securing the scissors hold. However, Lewis felt Stecher's legs circling his waist and flailed like a whirling dervish to get free.[xii]

The men began to warily circle each other again. Both men were perspiring freely.

Lewis rushed at Stecher, who grabbed a reverse arm lock and wrenched Lewis face first to the mat. Lewis' face betrayed serious pain before he wriggled free. Lewis grabbed his first headlock, which he used to throw Stecher to the mat. Stecher shot back to his feet quickly. It had taken Lewis 35 minutes to secure his first headlock.[xiii]

As advertised, the match was shaping up as Lewis' headlock versus Stecher's scissors hold. Who would score with their pet hold?

Ironically, it was a toe hold for both men, which almost ended the match.[xiv] Stecher secured a scissors hold on Lewis for the second time, but Lewis countered with a toe hold. Stecher almost submitted before spinning out of the toe hold.

Stecher took Lewis back to the mat with a reverse arm lock. Spinning to Lewis' back, Stecher was finally able to fully lock-in a scissors hold. After about a fifty second squeeze, Lewis looked close to submitting. Using speed not found in one built like "the Strangler," Lewis spun himself and created enough space to get out of the hold.

However, Lewis left a foot behind, which Stecher caught for a toe hold of his own. Lewis's face went grey as Stecher applied the pressure. Lewis reached back and cupped Stecher's face and started to pull him over backward. He was able to free his legs and he twisted his own body. It was the closest Lewis came to losing this match.

For the remainder of the match, Lewis went on the offensive. He secured his second headlock and threw Stecher to the mat. Stecher returned to his feet only for Lewis to throw Stecher back to the mat. This series went on for two or three throws before Stecher freed himself from the headlocks. Stecher was staggering around the ring from the effects of the headlock.

Lewis grabbed another headlock and threw Stecher to the mat. Stecher escaped the headlock with a head scissors.[xv] Lewis pulled free.

Stecher secured one more scissor hold but Lewis easily escaped by standing up and letting Stecher slide down their now sweat covered bodies back to the floor.

Stecher stood up only for Lewis to throw him back to the mat with a headlock. Stecher rose for one more headlock toss before succumbing for the pin fall after 1 hour, 37 minutes.[xvi] Ed "Strangler' Lewis was the new World Heavyweight Wrestling Champion. It would be the first of six title reigns.

To return to the question we asked earlier in the chapter, was this match a legitimate contest as Lewis later claimed. The coverage of the match indicates Lewis and Stecher were working with each other in a prearranged title switch.

First, Lewis used the headlock extensively in the match. Lewis would not use the headlock in a legitimate wrestling match.

The headlock is a painful hold, but it isn't dangerous. You aren't going to cut off the flow of blood to the head from this position. It is also highly unlikely that you will be able to force an opponent to submit from the pain.

Tactically though, you are giving your back to your opponent, when you secure the headlock. You are vulnerable to counter throws and submission holds. Early on in Brazilian Jiu-Jitsu classes, they will teach you to never use a headlock. Lou Thesz also says it is not a legitimate wrestling hold.[xvii]

The second reason I'm convinced Lewis and Stecher were working with each other was the amount of action in the match. It was a crowd-pleasing match to watch with lots of actions. Legitimate contests as a rule tend to be long, boring and many times inconclusive. With no time limits, the wrestlers stalemated most of the time fearful of their opponent countering them when they attempted a throw or hold.

Muldoon versus Whistler went to a 7-hour draw. The first Alex Aberg-Wladek Zbyszko match went almost four hours before declared a draw. The coverage in the newspaper consisted of one paragraph. We already wrote about the three contests between Stecher and Lewis, which took over 11 hours. The pace and action of this match illustrates the men were clearly working with each other.

Based on the real animosity between the two men, which looks to have been nothing more than professional jealousy, the match could have become a shoot but didn't. In the future, the old rivalry between the men would lead to double-crosses but in 1920 they buried the hatchet long enough to work together. Their cooperation would be short-lived.

Figure 7- Ed "Strangler" Lewis with one of his World Title Belts (Public Domain)

Chapter 2 – Ed "Strangler" Lewis First Title Reign

Sandow and Lewis started defending the title almost immediately. Lewis defended his title for the first time on January 24, 1921, at Madison Square Garden. They chose Earl Caddock, former World Heavyweight Wrestling Champion, as the opponent.[xviii]

Caddock won the title from Joe Stecher in a worked match in 1917. World War I interrupted his title reign as Caddock served in the U.S. Army during 1918 and 1919. Caddock dropped the title back to Stecher after completing his service commitment.

Figure 8- Earl Caddock from the Public Domain

While Caddock primarily took part in worked matches, he was more than capable of winning legitimate contests. A Lewis victory over Caddock would help firmly establish him as the top wrestler in the country.

Promoters selected Caddock because Joe Stecher was unavailable for a rematch. Whether he suffered the injury during the match or during training leading up to the match, Stecher was suffering neuritis in his right arm and shoulder.[xix]

Stecher attributed to his injury to the damaging effects of Lewis' headlock, but the headlock doesn't affect these areas of the body.[xx] However, when wrestlers suffered injuries, they often attribute them to their opponent to setup a rematch in the future. This practice continues today even though fans know professional wrestling is a work.

Stecher's physician, Dr. Edwards, told newspaper reporters that the injury would require Stecher to rest from wrestling and training for about a year.[xxi]

Caddock's manager Gene Melady claimed to have secured a $10,000 guarantee for the title match with Lewis.[xxii] We cannot trust these figures as many times promoters made them up to enhance the match hype as a major event. The wrestlers received a percentage of the gate, which was a further incentive to cooperate. Instead of receiving a bigger share for winning the match, the wrestlers would split a percentage evenly or based on their perceived drawing power.

Prior to the match with Caddock, Lewis took a tune-up match with local wrestler Jack Dawson in Columbia, South Carolina on January 15, 1921. Lewis beat Dawson in two straight falls.[xxiii]

Lewis also had victories over Stasia Padonney and Dick Daviscourt prior to the bout.[xxiv] Caddock didn't wrestle anyone as a tune-up for Lewis.

A few days before the bout, Billy Sandow cleverly dropped a story to the New York papers that Earl Caddock and his team tried to get the New York State Athletic Commission to ban Lewis' headlock. Caddock denied the assertion and reminded Sandow that Lewis submitted to Caddock's toehold, when Caddock was World Champion.[xxv]

The story was an obvious plant to increase interest in the match. If the match were a contest, the last thing Caddock would want banned is the headlock. Sandow was a consummate promoter and wanted to generate a heated rivalry to increase ticket sales.

Despite Jack Curley originally booking Madison Square Garden for the match, the 71st Regiment Armory was again the scene for this title match. It may have been a sign the promotion couldn't sell enough tickets to justify having the match at Madison Square Garden. While 8,000 fans attended the Stecher-Lewis match, only 7,000 fans attended this bout.[xxvi]

Lewis weighed between 223 and 228 pounds, while Caddock weighed between 185 and 190 pounds at 5'11".[xxvii]

For the first hour of the match, it was uneventful. Caddock looked to be the superior wrestler though. He put Lewis in his toehold, which had the champion on the verge of submission.[xxviii] Lewis was able to shake it off and get back to his feet.

At the one-hour mark, Caddock appeared to visibly tire. The weight difference between the two men seemed to be wearing on Caddock.[xxix]

Lewis secured his first headlock at about the 1 hour, 3-minute mark. He squeezed his left arm around Caddock's head and threw him to the mat. Charles F. Mathison writing for the *New York Herald* noted that Lewis put his last two major opponents, Joe Stecher and Wladek Zbyszko, in the hospital from the effects of the headlock.[xxx]

Lewis threw Caddock to the ground several times with the headlock before Caddock was able to grab Lewis' foot. Once again, Caddock started to apply the toehold, but Lewis broke it easier this time.[xxxi]

Lewis again secured the headlock and threw Caddock forcefully to the ground. Caddock struck his head and knocked himself insensible. Referee George Bothner registered the pin fall for Lewis. After several minutes, Caddock was able to get to his feet and shake hands with Lewis.[xxxii]

The hype around the headlock was successful as ringside fans began yelling, "No more headlocks!"[xxxiii] Sandow got the headlock over as one of the most dangerous holds in wrestling. Unfortunately for Sandow, he did too good of a job. Two days after the bout, the New York State Athletic Commission banned the headlock in New York City.[xxxiv]

Fred Hawthorne wrote about the match for the *New York Tribune*. On the major parts of the match, his coverage matched Mathison's article for the *Herald*. In some respects, including the wrestlers' bodyweight, their coverage didn't match.

We should expect variations in coverage. Prior to film and television, reporters watched the match live and wrote about them immediately afterwards. Even with immediately drafting the article with any notes, writers sometimes make errors in recalling match events without the benefit of film to check their recollections.

The headlock did not injure Caddock, who was near the end of his wrestling career. Caddock's career rise was meteoric with just as quick an exit from the profession.

Caddock started wrestling in 1915, won the World Title in 1917 and was retired by 1922. Sandwiched into these 7 years was a 2-year stint in the U.S. Army. Caddock could boast one of the most successful 5-year careers in American professional wrestling.

EARL CADDOCK.

Figure 9- Earl Caddock in Military Uniform in 1918 (Public Domain)

Caddock left wrestling to head back home to Walnut, Iowa, where he was successful in the automobile and oil businesses.[xxxv]

Caddock had a heart attack in 1948. He struggled with his health for the next two years. Another operation in 1950, left Caddock bed ridden.[xxxvi] He died two months later at 62 years of age with his wife by his side. His obituary referred to him as a prominent Southwest Iowa businessperson.[xxxvii]

Lewis was a long time from retirement. He began touring again as World Champion but the heat on the headlock was becoming an issue. In Kansas City, Lewis defended his title against Gustav Sulzo. Lewis used a double wristlock to win the first fall. During the second fall, Lewis threw Sulzo to the mat with the headlock for the deciding fall.[xxxviii]

As Sulzo lay on the mat unconscious, the Kansas City fans surrounded the ring. A squad of Kansas City police officers pushed the fans back and escorted Lewis to the dressing room. The fans screamed abuse and epithets at Lewis but didn't attack him.[xxxix] The Missouri Athletic

Commission was concerned with the fans' reaction.

Lewis defended his title against Renato Gardini in Boston on January 31, 1921. Promoters, not the athletic commission, banned the headlock in Boston. This ban was a promotional tactic, but it again drew attention to Lewis' headlock. Lewis used a toehold to defeat Gardini after 1 hour, 38 minutes.[x1]

Figure 10- Renato Gardini in 1924 (Public Domain)

On February 2, 1921, Lewis used the headlock to beat Billy Martinson in Portland, Maine.[xli] Lewis' schedule was brutal particularly considering most mass transit would have been by train.

On February 17th, Lewis returned to Kansas City for a potentially dangerous match with John "Tigerman" Pesek. Pesek disliked the worked nature of professional wrestling. Promoters were never sure, if Pesek would go along with prearranged finish. To use the headlock, Lewis would be giving Pesek his back and putting himself in a vulnerable position with a capable shooter in Pesek.

As a future incident between the men proved in the 1930s, Pesek was no match for Lewis, when he was past forty and legally blind. In 1921, Pesek must have known he was not on the same level as Ed "Strangler' Lewis.

Lewis used the headlock to win the match in two straight falls. Pesek laid on the mat for several minutes after the end of the second fall.[xlii] Once again, the Kansas City Police had to save Lewis from the enraged fans.

On February 23rd, Lewis was back in the state of New York. He wrestled the dangerous Dick Daviscourt in Rochester. The promoter banned the headlock for this match also. Lewis took the first fall after 1 hour, 45 minutes with a hammerlock and double wristlock. It took him only 17 minutes and 32 seconds to take the second fall with an arm and body hold.[xliii]

On February 27, 1921, the *Omaha Daily Bee* ran a story about a new challenge although it was more promotional than inside the ring. Tex Rickard, who promoted boxing's first million-dollar gate, decided to enter professional wrestling in New York. Rickard's move was a direct challenge to Jack Curley, Billy Sandow, and "Strangler" Lewis.[xliv]

Rickard had the money and connections with the state athletic commissions to challenge any wrestling promoters including the dominant faction headed by Billy Sandow. Rickard's challenge to Curley was a challenge to Sandow and Lewis also, since Curley aligned promotionally with Sandow's group.

Rickard was backing Marin Plestina, a skilled wrestler trained by Martin "Farmer" Burns, to challenge Lewis in a legitimate contest. Lewis was willing but Sandow was reluctant. Lewis would beat Plestina most nights of the week, but anything could happen in a legitimate contest. If Lewis were somehow injured and Plestina emerged victorious, Lewis' reputation would be severely damaged.

Figure 11-Marin Plestina from the Public Domain

Lewis was more than willing to wrestle Plestina, but Sandow and Curley weren't willing to put him in the ring. The challenge drug out for months. Finally, Sandow and Curley enlisted John "Tiger Man" Pesek to represent them.

In the ensuing contest to settle the promotional dispute, Pesek lost the match by being disqualification. Pesek wasn't worried about pinning or submitting Plestina, which Pesek could have done.

Instead, he continually fouled Plestina by palm striking him, hitting him with elbows and stuffing any offense Plestina attempted. The referee disqualified Pesek in two straight falls, but Pesek accomplished his assignment. By the end of the match, Pesek had made Plestina look so second rate that Tex Rickard announced his withdrawal from professional wrestling.

Curley and Sandow would use Pesek to see off another potential challenge in 1923 but this promotional would be an omen of future problems for Sandow's combination. Their success would make many enemies and lead to a falling out between Curley and Sandow themselves.

Figure 12- Ed "Strangler" Lewis and Billy Sandow in Lewis airplane from the April 29, 1921, Independence Daily Reporter (Public Domain) In the day when most traveled by train, Lewis' airplane was very handy for the touring World Champion.

Chapter 3 – The Old Man Returns from Europe

Prior to "Strangler" Lewis beating Joe Stecher for the World Title in December 1920, a major development for the wrestling promotion occurred earlier in the year. In February 1920, Stanislaus Zbyszko returned from Europe.

Stanislaus Zbyszko was well-known from his first tour wrestling in the United States between 1909 and 1914. Zbyszko left Poland to challenge Frank Gotch for the World Championship. After defeating all challengers during a 1910 tour of the United States, he wrestled Frank Gotch in a non-title match. Gotch was unable to throw him in 90-minutes setting up a world title match.

The title match was controversial. Gotch tackled Zbyszko off the customary handshake for a quick pin and first fall at 6 and a half seconds. Zbyszko threatened to walk out of the match demanding the referee wave the first fall off.

When the referee threatened to award the second fall and match to Gotch, Zbyszko reluctantly agreed to continue the match. Gotch won the second fall and match. Gotch would never wrestle Zbyszko again despite Zbyszko's status as the number one contender from 1910 to 1913. Gotch was the only wrestler able to defeat Zbyszko, albeit controversially, during Zbyszko's five-year tour.

Zbyszko wrestled a draw with Georg Hackenschmidt in 1911 in the hopes of forcing Gotch to wrestle him again. Gotch instead wrestled a rematch with Hackenschmidt, who Gotch beat for the World Championship in 1908.

Figure 13- Zbyszko around the Time of his 1910 Tour

Gotch retired in 1913 after a sporadic wrestling schedule in 1912 and 1913. Zbyszko remained in America until 1914, when he beat Aleksander "Alex" Aberg for the Greco-Roman Wrestling World Heavyweight Championship. Zbyszko didn't defend the title as frustration, and World War I interrupted his title reign.

Unable to secure a rematch with Gotch and not seeing any real challengers for the World Greco-Roman title, Zbyszko left for Poland in 1914. World War I soon trapped him in Europe. He spent some time in a prisoner of war camp before the end of the war led to his release. The war exiled Zbyszko in Europe for 6 years.

In early 1920, U.S. Senator J. Ham Lewis of Illinois took an interest in Zbyszko's attempts to return to America. Zbyszko was interested in raising money for the Polish Relief Fund, one of Colonel Lewis' pet projects.[xlv] Lewis helped Zbyszko obtain a passport to return to America.

On February 13, 1920, Stanislaus Zbyszko landed in New York on the Danish steamer *Oscar II*.[xlvi] New York promoter Jack Curley already had a match scheduled for Zbyszko on the following month's wrestling card.

One thing was evident from the moment Zbyszko stepped off the steamship. The World War I internment and his exile from competitive wrestling had aged him. While he would be turning forty on April

1st, Zbyszko could have passed for an in-shape 50-year-old.

Zbyszko still had the barrel chest and muscular development, but promoters often advertised him as being several years older. Promoters wanted to build his reputation as the "grand old man of wrestling."

"Strangler" Lewis and Stanislous Zbyszko

Figure 14- Lewis and Zbyszko Shake Hands before a match in 1921 (Public Domain)

Zbyszko was wrestling against Salvador Chevalier, who was supposed to have won an international tournament in Paris. Promoters often made up these victories as a promotional tactic. It was difficult, if not impossible, to prove whether such victories occurred.

Zbyszko ended up wrestling Frank Zolar instead of Salvador Chevalier. American professional wrestling had changed significantly by 1920. Zbyszko would have to adapt to the new style.

During his first tour of America during 1910 to 1914, Zbyszko wrestled primarily in legitimate contests. Zbyszko and Gotch may have been working together in the non-title match to build the world title match up. Otherwise, Zbyszko's wrestled shoot matches with his opponents during his first tour.

When he returned to the United States in 1920, American professional wrestling had changed from a mix of contests and exhibitions to matches being prearranged exhibitions. Occasionally, promoters would match up two shooters to settle a promotional war like when Pesek wrestled Plestina. Otherwise, wrestlers worked with each other in putting on exciting matches.

The only other legitimate contests were double-crosses when a wrestler stopped cooperating with his opponent. The double-crosser began wrestling legitimately to beat their opponent despite the previously agreed upon finish. Sometimes a promoter or manager was behind the double-cross.

Some wrestlers decided to beat an inferior opponent on their own. To prevent double-crosses, the promoters normally put titles only on legitimate wrestlers like Joe Stecher, Earl Caddock and Ed "Strangler" Lewis.

Zbyszko adapted to the new style and beat Zolar in two straight falls. He even used a headlock to win the first fall.[xlvii]

Zbyszko defeated a few more opponents before he found himself stuck in the middle of a promotional war, which would cause him to be inactive for most of 1920.

Prior to Pesek ending Tex Rickard's promotion of Marin Plestina, Zbyszko agreed to wrestle Plestina.[xlviii] Rickard and Plestina hoped to burnish their credentials for a Lewis challenge by defeating the wrestler, only Frank Gotch had beaten, albeit extremely controversially.

In hindsight, Curley and Sandow should have allowed the match to occur. Even at 40 years of age, Zbyszko would have cleanly pinned Plestina and ended the challenge of Rickard. However, they considered Zbyszko's acceptance of the match to be a betrayal.

Zbyszko would not receive any other bookings in 1920. While he may not have been aware of the promotional machinations, although the Curley-Sandow faction booked his younger brother Wladek Zbyszko, he quickly figured it out. The match with Plestina never occurred.

By early 1921, Stanislaus Zbyszko was back in good graces with Curley and Sandow. In fact, with his credentials, fans saw Stanislaus Zbyszko as one of the credible challengers for Ed "Strangler' Lewis.

When Zbyszko returned to the United States as we discussed earlier, he had aged. He had also put on significant weight. Zbyszko exited the Oscar II at 275 pounds, which was a lot of weight to carry on his 5'09" frame. After a year of serious training, he was back to his best wrestling weight of 230 pounds.[xlix]

On January 29, 1921, Zbyszko wrestled his first match since spring 1920, when he defeated Bob Monogoff (possibly Bobby Managoff, Sr.) in two straight falls in Laramie, Wyoming.[1]

Figure 15-Bob Managoff, Sr. (Public Domain)

Zbyszko's next match, in Milwaukee, Wisconsin, firmly established him as a contender for Lewis' title. Zbyszko defeated well-thought of veteran, and former American Heavyweight Champion, Charley Cutler in two straight falls. Zbyszko defeated Cutler with a double wristlock after 43 minutes, 50 seconds for the first fall. Zbyszko needed less than 7 minutes to throw Cutler for the second fall.[li]

Zbyszko returned to New York on Valentine's Day, February 14, 1921, in a preliminary match with John Freyberg. Jack Curley promoted the bout confirming what everyone already suspected. Stanislaus Zbyszko made peace with the dominant promotional group after the misstep of agreeing to wrestle Plestina.

In the publicity leading up to the match, Zbyszko's promoters and manager began to inflate his age to make his ring accomplishments seem even more impressive. The promotional team claimed Zbyszko was attempting a comeback at 45 years of age instead of his true age of forty.[lii] The promoters also mentioned his time spent in a German prisoner of war camp.

Zbyszko Working Out In Practice With Partner

In the picture, the world champion wrestler is shown on the right. He is using a double wrist lock on Steve Savage, one of his grappling mates

Figure 16-Stanislaus Zbyszko Training from the January 26, 1922, St. Louis Star and Times (Public Domain)

Zbyszko won the match with Freyberg in 29 minutes, 13 seconds with a toehold. Zbyszko kept working for the hold during the match and finally submitted him on the third toehold.[liii] Earl Caddock defeated Jim Londos, the biggest wrestling star of the 1930s, in the main event.

The *Arizona Republic* carried an article about Stanislaus Zbyszko's daily breakfast and lunch at a local San Francisco restaurant. For breakfast, he ate three grapefruit, six soft boiled eggs, a double portion of bacon and eggs and two quarts of milk. This meal was a light snack compared to lunch.[liv]

For lunch he had two heads of celery, half a salmon, double portion of porterhouse steak (enough for four people), a can of asparagus tips, two dishes of figs, two orders of rice pudding and two quarts of milk. Zbyszko's daily fare closed the restaurant one day because he ate all the day's inventory.[lv]

Promoters often placed such copy in newspapers to build the reputation of a wrestler. It isn't implausible though that Zbyszko may have eaten this much to support his wrestling and weight training.

Curley and Sandow were obviously building Zbyszko to challenge Ed "Strangler" Lewis. On March 14, 1921, Zbyszko wrestled with former World Champion Joe Stecher in New York City.

Stecher had not wrestled since his match with Lewis in December 1920. Stecher took time off to heal the neuritis in his arm. Whether he had a legitimate injury or just needed some time off from several years at the top of the wrestling cards, Stecher was ready to get back into the ring.

Curley announced a few weeks before the match that he banned only the stranglehold, which is what they were calling the headlock, for this match.[lvi] Since neither man really used the hold, it was an odd move to bar and once again brought attention to Lewis' pet hold.

By March 7, 1921, Zbyszko was in New York putting on public workouts for the fans with his brother Wladek at George

65

Bothner's gym. Pundits were impressed by Stanislaus' physical condition and noted he looked to be peaking a few days before the match.[lvii] The workouts drew a large crowd each day. Curley's pre-match hype looked to be drawing a good gate.

When the men entered the ring on March 14th, several thousand fans had crowded into the 71st Regiment Armory. As usual, former lightweight champion George Bothner was the assigned referee.

Figure 17- Wladek Zbyszko in 1917 (Public Domain)

The match would be a long one. For the first 90 minutes, Stecher dominated the match. Zbyszko used his strength to defend against Stecher's attacks.[lviii]

After 2 hour, 10 minutes, Stecher finally secured his scissors hold. Zbyszko's face showed the strain of the squeeze around his midsection. Bothner started to lean in as he expected Zbyszko to submit.[lix] However, Zbyszko squirmed free and secured a wrist and crotch hold.

When Zbyszko secured the crotch hold, he immediately lifted Stecher to shoulder height. After dumping Stecher to the mat, Zbyszko covered him for first and only fall for the win.[lx] Zbyszko and Stecher shook hands to end the match.

Zbyszko and Stecher would work together many times after this match. Their first outing proved to be a crowd pleaser.

Zbyszko was now a top contender for World Champion Ed Lewis. The man, who only lost to Frank Gotch, was set to wrestle the current World Champion. Could the soon-to-be 41-year-old Zbyszko finally become World Champion?

Photo by International Newsreel Corporation.

STANISLAUS ZBYSZKO OF CRACOW, POLAND.

Figure 18-Stanislaus Zbyszko in 1921 (Public Domain)

Chapter 4 – Zbyszko Wrestles Lewis

The match between Zbyszko and Lewis was set for May 6, 1921, at the 22nd Regiment Armory in New York City. Despite his advanced age, fans considered Zbyszko the first real threat to the title after beating Stecher two months earlier.

To hype the match, Lewis and Zbyszko appeared on the same card in Chicago on April 13th. Lewis defeated Jim Londos. Londos would avoid Lewis later in his career after Londos became a big star. Lewis took the only fall for a victory after 1 hour, 50 minutes. Lewis used six headlocks, including one lasting 5 minutes, to defeat Londos.[lxi]

Zbyszko defeated John "Tigerman Pesek in 1 hour, 20 minutes with a crotch hold and half-nelson. Leading into the match with Lewis, Zbyszko emphasized his Greco-Roman wrestling credentials by using Greco-Roman holds to finish his matches.

Part of the money from the Lewis-Zbyszko card would be going to the Irish Relief Fund.[lxii] The fund provided relief to women and children impacted by the Irish War of Independence.

On May 3, 1921, a major story started to make the rounds of the newspapers. Frank G. Menke of King Features Syndicate reported that the Curley faction booked Stanislaus to win the championship on May 6th as a reward for joining Jack Curley's combine.[lxiii] Menke said Zbyszko would win after about 2 hours, when it looked like Lewis was on the verge of victory.

Menke pointed out that Curley booked the dominant group of Lewis, Stecher, Earl Caddock and Wladek Zbyszko, who had traded the World Championship back and forth since 1915. Stanislaus sat in a European prisoner of war camp for most of this time. Menke's source was supposed to be a member of Curley's promotional office.[lxiv] Menke proved to be partially right.

7,500 spectators crowded into the 22nd Regiment Armory to watch the anticipated match. While Zbyszko was older, only Frank Gotch had beaten him. Fans thought he may be able to defeat new champion Lewis, who was becoming more unpopular all the time due to his use of the headlock.

After referee George Bothner provided final instructions, Lewis and Zbyszko shook hands before retiring to their corners to start the match. For the first fifteen minutes, both men used rough tactics in the tie-up.

Lewis grabbed a body hold after 4 minutes but Zbyszko shook it off. At 8 minutes, Lewis secured a toehold, which seemed to punish Zbyszko's legs.[lxv] Because of his bare feet, Lewis struggled to keep the hold on Zbyszko.

Things looked bad for Zbyszko until he wriggled to the edge of the mat after about 90 seconds. The referee ordered the Lewis to break the hold. The men returned to the center of the ring.[lxvi]

Lewis shocked Zbyszko and the crowd with his next move. Lewis caught the former Greco-Roman wrestling champion with a body hold and threw him over his shoulder.[lxvii] Considering Zbyszko's experience in the upper body throwing style, the one move no one expected to work against him was an upper body throw.

"Zibby" landed hard but didn't hit his shoulders. He jumped back to his feet. Zbyszko didn't appear winded from the throw but was obviously shocked. He approached Lewis carefully for the remainder of the match.

Zbyszko did get Lewis off his feet and tried to apply his own toehold, but Lewis rolled out of the hold. It was Zbyszko's only offense in the match.

Lewis went back on the offensive and secured a head scissors, but Zbyszko powered out of the potential submission.

After about 23 minutes of wrestling offensively, Lewis tried to apply his finisher. Lewis went to grab a flying headlock but due to Zbyszko's sweating and his tendency to pull his head towards his shoulders to make a smaller target, Lewis slipped off and fell to the mat.

It was the mistake Zbyszko had been looking for as he pounced on top of Lewis and used his 226-pounds to press the larger Lewis' shoulders to the mat for the only fall and victory.[lxviii] Stanislaus Zbyszko won the World Heavyweight Wrestling Championship 11 years after his last title shot.

The quickness of the turnaround and the shortness of the match shocked the crowd.[lxix] Championship matches lasting around 2 hours were the norm for spectators and pundits.

Due to the loose lips in Curley's office, the promotional team obviously needed to call an audible to prevent a significant exposure of professional wrestling.

Lewis did outwrestle Zbyszko throughout much of the match making the result appear to be a fluke. Several newspaper reports said Lewis was the superior wrestler, but Zbyszko used his experience to take advantage of "Lewis' mistake."[lxx]

Surprisingly, Lewis' first title reign lasted only 6 months from his defeat of long-time rival Joe Stecher to his loss to Zbyszko. Lewis never minded dropping the title because he could always take it back in a shoot.

Aleksander "Alex" Aberg sued Jack Curley over his time wrestling for Curley in 1916. The case came to trial in New York during 1917. Aberg exposed the worked nature of American wrestling during his testimony.

Aberg testified that as early as 1915, Ed "Strangler" Lewis would have to post a $250 bond as a promise he would not double-cross his opponent and beat him legitimately.[lxxi] Promoters thought 24-year-old Lewis could beat anyone in catch-as-catch-can wrestling. Jim Londos demanded a much bigger guarantee in the 1930s.

Such a short title reign was unexpected. Sandow and Lewis may have decided to take some heat off his finisher, the headlock, which state athletic commissions banned in some locations. 41-year-old Zbyszko, who promoters billed as forty-six, was running out of time as a potential title holder, so it made sense to make the title switch, while he was hot. Curley could also have been flexing his muscle with his partners, who did not agree with the title change. We'll never know the real reason for the short title reign.

For Zbyszko, he was now the World Champion. How long would it last though?

Figure 19-"Strangler" Lewis using a front face lock on Ivan Linow in 1920

Chapter 5 – The Old Man as Champion

Based on how he won the title, most observers expected Zbyszko to have a short reign. He had a great story, but it was both a blessing and a curse.

Zbyszko's accomplishments were legendary. Zbyszko was the only man to defeat Alex Aberg in Greco-Roman wrestling during Aberg's tour of America. Zbyszko's undefeated record also included almost no worked matches. Zbyszko was as close to undefeated in legitimate contests as any wrestler in history.

Winning the world title at 41 years of age, after being a prisoner of war, was also a great story. Several newspapers ran stories about his wartime experiences in the weeks following his championship victory. Age was the biggest aspect of his story though.

In an interview with Newspaper Enterprises, Zbyszko told the writer,

"There is no sense in getting old. To do so is very unintelligent. If you would stay young and virile, you must exercise more and eat much less."[lxxii]

The same article attributed 927 straight victories to Zbyszko. Zbyszko said he expected to be better physically at 60 than he was at the time of the article.[lxxiii]

Figure 20-Stanislaus Zbyszko in the Idaho Statesman from 1921 (Public Domain)

While it is a nice sentiment, anyone reading the article knows that Father Time is the one opponent no one can beat. At some time, your skills and physical condition begin to diminish. In this respect, his age was also a curse.

Fans were only going to take Zbyszko seriously as a World Champion for so long before they began to question the legitimacy of his victories. From the time he won the title, the clock was ticking on how long promoters would let him carry the championship.

One of Zbyszko's first title defenses was a rematch with Joe Stecher in Kansas City, Missouri. The match occurred on May 26th. Zbyszko beat Stecher in two straight falls.[lxxiv]

The first fall took Zbyszko almost two hours to gain. Zbyszko won the second fall in 13 minutes. Promoters pushed Zbyszko strongly in this match.

The next night, Zbyszko was in Wichita, Kansas to wrestle Nick Daviscourt. Zbyszko beat Daviscourt for the first fall in 47 minutes. He won the second fall from Daviscourt in 5 minutes.[lxxv]

In a transportation feat as air travel was in its infancy, Zbyszko was in Boston on May 30th to defeat Pete Daily in a one fall match.[lxxvi]

On June 3, 1921, in Philadelphia, Pennsylvania, Zbyszko defended his title against Ivan Linow at the Metropolitan Opera House. The charity match raised money for French war relief. Zbyszko beat Linow with a toehold after 59 minutes, 13 seconds.[lxxvii]

Zbyszko was in Philadelphia on June 11th to wrestle William Demetral. Zbyszko beat Demetral with a toehold and arm lock in 61 minutes.[lxxviii] In the same article, the reporter announced a Zbyszko-Lewis rematch on June 27th in New York City.

On June 23rd though, Curley announced the rematch was off. Ed "Strangler" Lewis called the match off because both men were supposed to get 40% of the gate. He felt he should have a larger percentage.[lxxix] Lewis was positioning himself as a heel for the rematch.

Figure 21-Jack Demspey and Stanislaus Zbyszko on a Los Angeles Beach in 1922 (Public Domain)

During the summer, the Zbyszko brothers received word that their mother was gravely ill. Making quick preparation, they let Curley and the other promoters know they would be leaving as soon as they could arrange passage on a ship.

They were able to book passage for Poland in the first week of July. They scheduled their return trip to the United States at the end of September.[lxxx] The return was an estimate as ship travel wasn't always easy to predict. Their mother's health would also be a primary driver for when they returned. Sadly, she passed away during their visit.

Upon their return from Poland, Stanislaus Zbyszko defended his title against former World Champion Earl Caddock. Zbyszko also made news by accepting a challenge through his manager.

Before leaving for Poland, Zbyszko's manager Jack Herman said Stanislaus Zbyszko would defend his title against the challenge of Marin Plestina sometime after the match with Caddock. Tex Rickard was still offering $25,000 for anyone to wrestled Plestina.[lxxxi]

Joe Marsh, who managed Plestina, correctly expressed doubt that the match would ever occur. "You can bet all the money in the United States of America that Herman will never doing anything of the sort – not while Zbyszko holds the Jack Curley championship."[lxxxii]

Marsh had a better understanding of the situation than either Herman or Stanislaus Zbyszko. Curley nor Sandow would ever let their World Champion wrestle a contest with Plestina even if the champion were likely to win.

The Zbyszkos did not return to the United States until October 1921, so his Des Moines, Iowa title defense on October 19, 1921, moved to November 7th in the same city.

In his first title defense back in the country, Zbyszko convincingly won in two straight falls. After 1 hour, 20 minutes, Zbyszko stood up with Caddock across his back and shoulders. Zbyszko threw himself backwards on top of Caddock for the first fall.[lxxxiii]

Caddock appeared injured and exhausted after the first fall. It took 24 more minutes, but Zbyszko took the second fall, when Caddock was unable to continue.[lxxxiv] Promoters were booking Zbyszko as a strong champion.

On November 12th, Zbyszko met Light Heavyweight Wrestling Champion Clarence Eklund in Sheridan, Wyoming. Zbyszko weighed 232 pounds and Eklund weighed 173 pounds. Due to their great weight disparity, Zbyszko agreed to throw Eklund twice in one hour or Eklund would win the match.

Eklund played defense for the first 45 minutes, but Zbyszko eventually grabbed hold of Eklund. Zbyszko fell on Eklund as he threw him to the ground for the first fall.[lxxxv] Eklund appeared too injured to continue, so the referee declared Zbyszko the winner.

Zbyszko frequently defended the title in New York City, but the New York State Athletic Commission threw a wrench into the works for a couple of wrestlers.

The Commission believed Curley's hype about the recent staged contests, upheld the ban on the headlock. They also added Joe Stecher's leg scissors to the list of banned holds.[lxxxvi]

Although they may have had suspicions, promoters did not smarten up most athletic commissions to the worked nature of professional wrestling. Promoters feared a credible source revealing that wrestlers worked matches would destroy their business.

Since Athletic Commissions could not be sure about pro wrestling's worked nature, they treated the matches as real. If a hold seemed particularly dangerous, they would often ban it. These bans made booking some matches more difficult.

The first Zbyszko-Lewis title rematch occurred on Monday night, November 28, 1921, in New York City's Madison Square Garden. The bigger venue in America's largest city made sense for the big rematch.

Despite the ban on the headlock, the New York State Athletic Commission provided a waiver for this match. Lewis could use the headlock.[lxxxvii] They banned carotid artery chokes only.

The referee would not be George Bothner but Johnny Fleeson. The bout would be controversial because the men wrestled under a new rule set. If one of the wrestler's shoulders touched the mat even during the process of an escape, they would lose the fall.[lxxxviii]

The fans did not understand these new rules as no one explained the rules in the pre-match newspaper coverage. As a result, the crowd was furious over how the match unfolded.

Unlike the normal two-hour matches of the time, this match was another quick bout. In under an hour, the wrestlers scored all three falls.

Lewis entered the ring first. At 237 pounds, the challenger was in excellent condition. Zbyszko entered the ring at his typical 232 pounds.

The match started quickly. The new rules would come into play at the 17-minute mark. Lewis secured a flying headlock and tossed Zbyszko to the mat. Zbyszko rolled through the throw but because his shoulders barely touched the match, Fleeson awarded Lewis the first fall.[lxxxix]

Zbyszko seemed confused at the quick fall. At the start of the second fall, Zbyszko went after Lewis belying his advanced age. Zbyszko secured one of his favorite lifts, the crotch hold, and started to turn Lewis towards the mat. Lewis rolled through the throw, but his shoulders touched the mat enough for Fleeson to award Zbyszko the second fall at 21 minutes.[xc]

The fans booed the decision lustily as Lewis put on his purple robe. Lewis started to leave the ring to protest the decision. Depending on which version you believe, either members of the Athletic Commission or his friends convinced him to continue the match.

The third fall was not controversial. Zbyszko was able to secure a double arm lock and force Lewis' shoulders to the mat after 14 minutes and 56 seconds.[xci]

Zbyszko had beaten Lewis a second time but again the outcome proved controversial. The flying falls looked fluky and helped both Lewis and Zbyszko look strong to the fans.

At some point, Zbyszko was going to have to drop the belt back to Lewis. He was enjoying his championship reign while it lasted.

Figure 22-Stanislaus Zbyszko in the San Francisco Chronicle from early 1921 (Public Domain)

Chapter 6 – Lewis Pursues Zbyszko

Zbyszko knew when he became World Champion that he would have to drop the belt back to Lewis. He didn't know when though.

Before any title switch, Sandow would have to hype the rematch. In December 1921, a story appeared in several newspapers to forward the promotion of the Zbyszko-Lewis program along.[xcii]

Since newspaper were the mass media of the day, Sandow could try a couple of tactics to get the coverage he wanted in the newspapers. He could try to interest journalists in a good story, which was the easiest way to place a promotional story. Failing that, Sandow could pay a journalist to plant the story. I'm not sure how the reporter compiled this story, but he wrote an interest piece on Stanislaus Zbyszko's love of opera music.

Even though he calls him a "pug" in the headline, the article was very complimentary of Zbyszko. It also quoted Zbyszko extensively.

The article starts with Zbyszko's formula for success. "My rules for success are determination, unswerving purpose, self-denial and hard work."[xciii]

Zbyszko was a regular at opening nights of the Metropolitan Opera. Zbyszko said music was compatible with athletic endeavors. "Opera helps me wrestle. Music is beautiful and every man, no matter what he is or does, must have something beautiful to help him through life. Music is my help. It gives me high ideals. Perhaps you think wrestlers do not need high ideals. But you are wrong."

Figure 23-Stanislaus Zbyszko in 1919 (Public Domain)

"Both my little brother, Wladek, and myself have made a study of various branches of music and harmony. We number among our friends quite a few grand opera stars. The late Enrico Caruso used often to enjoy a quiet game of chess with me."

"Wladek and I have many hot arguments about musical technique."

"When I was a little boy I began to have a liking for the better kind of music. I said then, 'I will never be old,' and in 60 years from now I shall still be young."[xciv]

Although he completed his law studies at the university, professional wrestling appealed to Zbyszko and he never practiced law.[xcv] The article painted Zbyszko as a cultured gentlemen in contrast to the normal roughneck, who plied their trade in professional wrestling.

To keep building towards a rematch, Zbyszko faced a significant challenge to begin 1922. Zbyszko wrestled Earl Caddock, former World Heavyweight Wrestling Champion, for the title on February 6, 1922, in Madison Square Garden.

The undercard would consist of Ed "Strangler" Lewis versus Renato Gardini as well as former Olympic wrestler and NCAA Champion Nat Pendleton wrestling Wladek Zbyszko. Sandow would take a major step forward to the title switch with this card.

Johnny Fleeson would again be the referee in the main event. Still feeling heat for the Zbyszko-Lewis rematch in November, Fleeson granted an interview in December 1921.[xcvi]

His interview caused more controversy as he said American wrestlers were deficient in bridging, which made them more susceptible to the "flying fall rule." Fleeson said only Greco-Roman wrestlers really bridged well because of the focus on upper body throws and falls.[xcvii]

American wrestlers skilled in catch wrestling focused more on submission holds instead of throws. As they weren't often subject to a rolling throw unless they met a Greco-Roman wrestling specialist, catch wrestlers didn't spend a lot of time bridging. At least it was Fleeson's story, and he was sticking to it.

"One advantage of the rolling fall rule will be the scampering of a lot of our grapplers to gymnasiums to take a few lessons in holds and escapes via the bridge or stomach roll."[xcviii]

12,000 fans crowded into Madison Square Garden to watch the match between the current and former champion.[xcix] One of the common stories about Zbyszko's title reign was he didn't draw big houses, so promoters had to switch the title back to Lewis. However, Zbyszko did draw big crowds for his title defenses against Caddock and Lewis.

Zbyszko weighed an official 223 for the bout although many spectators thought he weighed over 230 pounds. Promoters billed Caddock at 190 pounds, but he appeared lighter. While Zbyszko had a big size advantage, Caddock was almost 10 years younger as he would be thirty-four on February 27th.[c] Zbyszko would be 42 in April, but many claims still had his age between 46 and 49.

When the match started, Caddock took the offensive. Caddock secured an arm lock, but Zbyszko used his great strength to break the hold.[ci]

Caddock then attempted a leg scissors, but Zbyszko stood up and walked out of the hold. Zbyszko secured his first hold by grabbing a half-Nelson and trying to turn Caddock. However, Caddock wriggled free.

Zbyszko grabbed a second half-Nelson and started to turn Caddock, who rolled out of the hold. Or so he thought.

Both men were on their knees and rolled to their feet, when referee John Fleeson tapped Zbyszko on the back. Zbyszko looked confused and asked, "What happened?"[cii]

Fleeson awarded him the first fall due to the new "flying fall rule." Fleeson said both of Caddock's shoulders touched the mat as he rolled through the escape. The fans nearly rioted over the call.[ciii]

For the full 10-minute intermission, the fans continued to boo the decision. The *New York Herald* said several fans opined that Fleeson was standing at the time and could not have seen both shoulders touch the mat.[civ] Police surrounded the ring, but the fans didn't attack Fleeson.

When the men returned to the center of the ring, Caddock grabbed Zbyszko and took him to the mat. He went for an arm scissors on Zbyszko but failed to secure it. After a few more minutes of Zbyszko being on the defensive, Caddock applied an arm lock and threw Zbyszko to the mat with an impressive show of strength.[cv] Caddock won the second fall in 10 minutes, 20 seconds.

Zbyszko appeared shocked that Caddock was able to throw him. As both men started the third fall, the crowd was on edge anticipating a title change.

Zbyszko was able to secure one of his pet holds, the crotch hold, which he used to turn Caddock upside down. Caddock was trying to bridge to keep his shoulders from touching, but Fleeson again awarded a flying fall saying Caddock's shoulders rolled across the mat.[cvi]

The fans went from angry to crazed. Police removed Fleeson from the ring quickly to prevent a riot. The fans booed until the wrestlers left the area as well. After drawing such a large crowd, they sent them home angry. Promoters had to be careful with angles. If the crowd were too angry, they wouldn't come back. It was a delicate balancing act, which getting wrong could cost serious money.[cvii]

On the undercard, Ed "Strangler" Lewis defeated Renato Gardini in two straight falls using his headlock. Lewis was becoming the logical number one contender due to his two controversial losses to Zbyszko and current win streak. Around this time, Frank G. Menke through another wrench into the promotional machine.

According to Menke, the famous sportswriter for the Hearst newspapers, who broke the news of Lewis losing to Zbyszko, a title switch was imminent.[cviii] Menke said Jack Curley would soon switch the title from Zbyszko to former World Champion Joe Stecher.

Menke said the original choice to replace Zbyszko was John "Tigerman" Pesek. However, Pesek took part in a legitimate contest with Marin Plestina to settle a promotional war between Curley and Tex Rickard.

Instead of trying to defeat him, Pesek fouled Plestina for three straight falls, losing all of them by disqualification. The New York State Athletic Commission was so angry, they banned Pesek permanently from New York.[cix]

Figure 24-John "Tigerman" Pesek from the Public Domain

Menke said the public was tired of the triumvirate of Earl Caddock, Joe Stecher and Wladek Zbyszko as World Champion. Stanislaus Zbyszko was a welcome change for wrestling fans and his title reign drew big crowds before and after his trip to Poland. However, Curley, and the promoters aligned with him, liked to switch the belt every 12 to 18 months. Menke predicted Zbyszko would lose the belt to Stecher in mid-March, if not sooner.[cx]

Menke obviously had a source close to Jack Curley's promotional group. Until I read this article, I never found any source saying Stecher was supposed to replace Zbyszko. If it is true, it could explain the events of 1925. Was Stecher promised the title to have the opportunity taken away because of the Menke article and inter-promotional strife?

Lewis only had one match in 1922 prior to his defeat of Gardini. He threw Dick Daviscourt in two straight falls in Wichita, Kansas on January 7, 1922. He won the first fall in 24 minutes with his headlock. He won the second fall in 26 minutes with a grapevine.[cxi]

Lewis' next match in New York, after defeating Gardini, occurred two weeks later on February 22, 1922. Lewis defeated Clifford Binkley in two straight falls. Lewis took the first fall after 9 minutes. It took Lewis 28 minutes to score the second fall.[cxii]

A surprise occurred at the top of the card. Wladek Zbyszko, the younger brother of the current champion, defeated the handpicked successor Joe Stecher in a two out of three falls main event.[cxiii] If Curley and his group had intended to switch the belt to Stecher, they changed their minds by this card. Menke changed their mind.

Lewis again emerged as the leading contender to beat Zbyszko. Promoters booked Lewis to wrestle Zbyszko in Wichita, Kansas on March 6, 1922. Would Lewis regain the title?

Figure 25- Dick Daviscourt from the Public Domain

Chapter 7 – Lewis Regains the Championship

Lewis and Zbyszko met in Wichita on March 6th for the World Heavyweight Wrestling Championship. While it wasn't New York City, Wichita had a population of 72,000. It was also a town Sandow was looking to develop. However, neither fans nor reporters suspected a title switch here. A controversial victory for the champion was the likely outcome going into the match.

Zbyszko started the match with a strong offense. He even appeared dominant at times. Zbyszko won the first fall in 41 minutes, 30 seconds with an arm bar and body scissors.[cxiv]

Zbyszko continued to show superior skill in the match but was surprised by Lewis 17 minutes into the second fall. Zbyszko had applied an arm lock when Lewis spun around and shoved Zbyszko to the mat. Lewis leaped onto the prone Zbyszko to secure his headlock.[cxv] Lewis ground the headlock for a minute forcing Zbyszko's shoulders to the mat. Lewis scored the second fall at 18 minutes, 30 seconds.[cxvi]

Zbyszko struggled to his feet appearing dazed and confused. When the bell rang to start the third fall, Zbyszko could barely stand.

In his weakened state, Zbyszko was no match for Lewis, who threw him with another headlock at 3 minutes of the third fall. With little fanfare, Lewis had regained the World Championship he lost 10 months prior.[cxvii] Zbyszko lost only his second match during his time in America.

Zbyszko and his manager claimed the shove during the second fall was a closed fist punch.[cxviii] They accepted the referee's decision though.

The circumstances around the title change gives credence to Menke's article in early February 1922. The promotional group seemed determined to make a title change but after the Menke article, Joe

Stecher couldn't be the champion without exposing pro wrestling. Instead, the promotional partners selected Lewis to regain the title.

Curley and Sandow were always nervous Zbyszko would refuse to go along with a title switch. Even at Zbyszko's age, Lewis felt Zbyszko had the ability to legitimately defeat him in a contest. Lewis was the only wrestler able to manage Zbyszko during a double-cross but even he would have to be careful.

Zbyszko didn't try a double-cross. Lewis must have known Zbyszko was sincere. If Lewis suspected a double-cross, he would not have used the headlock.

Lewis and Zbyszko would have a rematch in the future, but Lewis didn't let grass grow under his feet in defending his title. On March 7, 1922, Lewis was in Indianapolis defending his title against John Grandovich.

Figure 26-John Grandovich from the Public Domain

Lewis met the 5-year veteran at the Broadway Theater in a match observers said was the best seen in the city.[cxix] Grandovich stood 5'11" and weighed 223 pounds, close to the same size as the champion. Grandovich used an arm lock on the champion for the first 30 minutes.[cxx]

Despite his early success, Grandovich would soon fall victim to Lewis' pet hold. Lewis secured the headlock and began taking Grandovich down with the headlock throw. Three times Lewis took him to the ground, but

Grandovich escaped each time. On the fourth throw, the impact knocked Grandovich senseless. Lewis took the first fall in 52 minutes.[cxxi]

Grandovich appeared compromised to begin the second fall. It was only a matter of time before Lewis scored the second fall. Instead of using a headlock, Lewis applied an arm bar and scissors to put Grandovich onto his back. Grandovich bridged for 4 minutes but Lewis pinned him at the 14-minute mark.[cxxii] Lewis won in two straight falls. Lewis looked as strong as ever.

On March 12th or 13th, Lewis was in Lexington, Kentucky to defend his title against New England Champion George "Farmer" Bailey. Lewis again won in two straight falls. Lewis used twelve headlocks to pin Bailey for the first fall in 46 minutes. It only took a minute for Lewis to win the second fall with an arm grapevine.[cxxiii]

On March 16, 1922, Lewis and his manager Billy Sandow made news by depositing $5,000.00 with the Sporting Editor of the *Nashville Banner* for a potential boxer vs. wrestler match with current World Heavyweight Boxing Champion Jack Dempsey.[cxxiv] Dempsey also seemed interest in the mixed match.

Dempsey would not wear gloves and could box or wrestle. Lewis would only be able to wrestle.[cxxv] Despite the mutual interest in what would have been a huge gate, the match never came off.

Lewis traveled to Topeka, Kansas for a March 24th match with Joe Geshtout, a Bulgarian grappler. 1,800 fans attended the double bill at the City Auditorium.[cxxvi] The championship bout was short.

Lewis caught Geshtout with the headlock throw for the first fall at 20 minutes. After a 10-minute intermission, Lewis only needed two minutes to pin Geshtout with an arm scissors and double wristlock.[cxxvii] Despite the short championship match for the time, the fans left the auditorium happy after seeing the champion's dominant performance.

Lewis made his first big title defense in Wichita, Kansas on April 13, 1922. Earl Caddock, the former world champion, wrestled Lewis in one of the final bouts of his short career.

Unlike previous contenders, Lewis would not beat Earl Caddock in two straight falls. In fact, Caddock won the first fall after 16 minutes with a head scissors.[cxxviii]

Lewis came back in the second fall by securing his headlock on Caddock after 43 minutes of hard wrestling. As usual in Lewis' matches, Caddock appeared weakened to begin the third fall. He again fell victim to the headlock after 8 minutes.[cxxix]

Lewis continued to roll in the shorter matches, which was a hit with the crowd. The reporter again noted the Caddock match was shorter than normal, but the crowd left happy.

Lewis' next big match was a puzzler. With very little fanfare, Lewis had his first rematch with former champion Stanislaus Zbyszko. They met in Kansas City, Missouri's Convention Hall to a near capacity crowd.[cxxx]

In the future, 12,000 fans would attend matches at Convention Hall. This crowd was between 9,000 and 12,000 showing Lewis' and Zbyszko's drawing power in the Midwest.

The match itself followed a similar formula. Lewis captured the first fall at 32 minutes with the headlock. Zbyszko won the second fall at 12 minutes with a wristlock and head scissors. Lewis captured the final fall and the match at 26 minutes with another headlock.[cxxxi]

Good results despite the lack of publicity. You can see how different the publicity was for this match by comparing this build-up to the build-up for the second match at the end of 1922.

As early as May 1922, Zbyszko was offering Lewis $20,000 for a finish rematch.[cxxxii] Zbyszko also offered to let Lewis keep the gate to secure a rematch. Zbyszko was trying to convince the fans about how seriously he was pursuing the rematch.

Figure 27-Ed "Strangler" Lewis demonstrating his headlock on an opponent (Public Domain)

Zbyszko didn't get his finish match yet, but Lewis did agree to meet him in Tulsa, Oklahoma in a ballpark. The match would have a two-hour time limit instead of being a finish match.[cxxxiii] The match would be two out of three falls or to the time limit.

The controversial "flying fall" rule, only legal in New York, would create controversy in this match. Dick Daviscourt, an active wrestler, was the referee for the match. Daviscourt was not an experienced referee. Daviscourt had wrestled both Lewis and Zbyszko in title matches but had little to recommend him as a referee for this match.

Lewis and Zbyszko wrestled an action-packed match until the 1 hour, 28-minute mark. Lewis' 10th headlock took Zbyszko to the mat. Daviscourt tapped Lewis on the back to signal his winning the first fall.

Zbyszko looked stunned and kicked the bottom rope. The fans began throwing their seat cushions into the ring to show their disdain for Daviscourt's decision. They screamed it was a flying fall and illegal in Oklahoma.[cxxxiv] The fans thought a wrestler would have to hold his opponent's shoulders to the mat to win the match.

Daviscourt refused to change his decision. Zbyszko challenged Daviscourt to an immediate match during the intermission. Zbyszko said he would throw him in 3 minutes. Daviscourt refused as the crowd jeered.[cxxxv]

Zbyszko was clearly becoming the fan favorite, while Lewis was the heel in this rivalry. Lewis returned to the ring after the 10-minute intermission.

Neither man was able to score another fall before the expiration of the two hours. The referee declared Lewis the winner based on his single fall over Zbyszko.

Lewis spent the remainder of the year beating a bunch of generic contenders leading into his last rematch with Stanislaus Zbyszko to take place in St. Louis, Missouri on Thursday, December 14, 1922. The controversy over the "flying fall" decisions would play into the build-up.

In early December, Lewis and Zbyszko both threatened to call the match off, if they were not satisfied with the referee selection. Zbyszko seemed to be smarting over the flying falls, he felt the referee unjustly awarded to Lewis.

Lewis may have been concerned with a double-cross, which would be much easier with the referee conspiring with his opponent. A promoter and wrestler double-crossed Lewis this way in 1931.

Promoter John Contos was able to allay the fears of both men with his selection. George Baptiste, a prominent local businessperson, and former nationally ranked middleweight wrestler was the chosen referee. Baptiste was known for his integrity. As the owner of Baptiste Tent and Awning, a successful St. Louis firm founded by his father Alexander, bribes did not tempt George Baptiste, who was a true athlete.

Besides his wrestling accomplishments, Baptiste saved at least three local swimmers, who the current in the Mississippi River overwhelmed. Contos felt Baptiste was the best choice for the job.

In a conference between Contos, Billy Sandow and Zbyszko's manager Jack Herman on December 10th, all men agreed Baptiste was a suitable choice. The match was on.[cxxxvi] The controversy didn't hurt the build-up of the match either.

10,000 fans crowded the St. Louis Coliseum for the big rematch. The *St. Louis Star-Times* reported the match attracted international interest.[cxxxvii]

The match started fast with both men demonstrating great skill. At the 18-minute mark, Lewis secured a toe hold after using a go-behind move. Lewis would drop to the floor, spin, and end up behind his opponent's legs. Lewis would then trip the man and attempt to secure a toehold.[cxxxviii] Zbyszko pulled Lewis' head back to escape and scrambled to his feet.

Zbyszko secured a double wrist lock and almost forced Lewis' shoulders to the mat. With only inches to go, Lewis rolled out of the hold and regained his feet.[cxxxix]

Lewis then applied three consecutive headlocks, all of which Zbyszko broke free from. On the third headlock, Lewis landed on the mat in a sitting position with Zbyszko behind him.

Lewis reached up and grabbed a flying mare. Lewis used the move to flip Zbyszko over his shoulders. Zbyszko landed on his knees, grabbed Lewis, who had started to stand up behind him, in the same hold. Zbyszko flipped Lewis, who landed sideways instead of on his knees.

Zbyszko pounced onto Lewis using his bodyweight to force Lewis' back to the floor. Zbyszko won the first fall with a flying mare at the 41-minute mark.[cxl]

Lewis made a comeback during the second fall. After securing two headlocks, Lewis again forced Zbyszko to the floor and applied a toehold. Zbyszko resisted the toehold for a full 4 minutes before reversing the hold.[cxli] One of

Zbyszko's main reasons for wrestling barefoot was because it helped him escape leg locks.

Lewis secured a second toehold, which Zbyszko broke out of after 2 minutes. Suitably weakening the challenger, Lewis grabbed Zbyszko in a flying headlock. Zbyszko slammed hard to the mat allowing Lewis to pin him.[cxlii]

Zbyszko appeared injured as his right arm hung at his side. After the intermission, Lewis immediately started working on the injured limb.

Lewis secured headlock after headlock taking Zbyszko to the ground repeatedly. Lewis then applied a hammerlock on Zbyszko's right arm. Yelling out in excruciating pain, Zbyszko submitted to the hold.[cxliii] Lewis was still World Heavyweight Wrestling Champion.

The match was a huge success. The paid gate was $16,000.00. Sixty percent of the gate was allocated to Lewis and Zbyszko. Lewis was supposed to have earned $7,200.00. Zbyszko took the loser's purse of $2,400.00.[cxliv] I'm not sure how they divided the gate, but these were the reported numbers to the Missouri Athletic Commission.[cxlv]

Ed "Strangler" Lewis closed out 1922 by going home to San Jose. His wife, Ida Morton Lewis, a female surgeon drained some fluid off a wrist injury.[cxlvi] Lewis was home to celebrate the holidays with his wife and daughter.

Lewis also reportedly signed a mixed match with Jack Dempsey over the holidays. However, the match never came off. It would have been a big financial payday, but Lewis would have plenty of opportunities for big pay offs over the next few years.

1922 had been a successful year for Lewis. Besides regaining the World Title, Lewis made good money even though he only had three big matches with Earl Caddock and four matches with Stanislaus Zbyszko.

Lewis wrestled in front of big crowds throughout the Midwest, which was becoming his base of operations. He only wrestled a couple matches in New York and on the East Coast.

The biggest development for Lewis personally, as well as professionally, was the edition of a young Colorado wrester into his training camp late in 1922. Joseph "Toots" Mondt would prove to be Lewis' best training partner, closest confidant, and most trusted business associate.

Mondt's mind for the business would also prove a boon to manager and promoter Billy Sandow. The team of Sandow, Lewis and Mondt were about to become "The Gold Dust Trio." The Trio would dominate pro wrestling in the mid-1920s.

Figure 28-Stanislaus Zbyszko from a December issue of the St. Louis Star and Times (Public Domain)

Chapter 8 – Joseph "Toots" Mondt

In 1922, Joseph "Toots" Mondt was 26-years old. Trained for professional wrestling by Martin "Farmer" Burns, Mondt was an accomplished wrestler, but Burns felt Mondt had even a better mind for the business.

Burns knew Mondt would eventually move into promotion because of his genius for match finishes, promotional angles and creating a more exciting form of wrestling in the ring.

Prior to joining the Gold Dust Trio in late 1922, Mondt was working with Burns' troupe and putting over wrestlers in their home territories. Mondt created a way to put over the wrestlers, while appearing tough and heroic at the same time. He used one of these finishes for the first time in 1922 during an April match with Ad Santel in Santel's hometown of San Francisco.

Figure 29-Ad Santel from the Public Domain

Born in Germany, Santel began his wrestling career as a protégé of Georg Hackenschmidt under his real name of Adolph Ernst. By the mid-1910s, he was using the name Ad Santel exclusively. Santel had a deserved reputation as both a shooter and hooker.

One of the legends around professional wrestling is Frank Gotch paid Santel $5,000 to purposely injure Hackenschmidt prior to his 1911 rematch with Gotch. Gotch took the world championship from Hackenschmidt in 1908.

I do not believe Gotch would pay Santel to injure someone he beat convincingly a couple years earlier, but the story has prevailed.[cxlvii] Santel was capable of injuring people as he demonstrated a few years later, which is why the legend had credence.

Santel specialized in taking on Judo black belts in legitimate contests of "wrestling versus jujitsu" in the mid-1910s. Santel ended all the bouts by injuring his opponent with a submission hold or slam.

Even though Santel wrestled in mostly worked wrestling matches, he had a short temper and mean streak. If he felt a wrestler was taking liberties, Santel would legitimately injure them like Evan "Strangler" Lewis in the 19th Century. Fans were aware of Santel's reputation, which helped make Mondt's angle believable.

Mondt wrestled Santel for an hour in the April 25th match before Santel secured a toehold. Santel held the hold for several minutes before Mondt submitted at the 1 hour, 6-minute mark to score the first fall.[cxlviii]

The match stopped for the 10-minute intermission. When the referee called for the 2-out-of-3-falls match to continue, the doctor would not let Mondt continue. The doctor stated Mondt had torn ligaments in his ankle. Despite protests from Mondt, the referee stopped the match and awarded to Santel.[cxlix]

When Mondt reentered the ring in early May to defeat Renato Gardini, the early return revealed he had worked the injury.[cl] The fans didn't seem to be any the wiser. Mondt would use the injury angle again during the rematch with Gardini.

In the rematch, Gardini and Mondt would wrestle a 2-out-of-three fall match. Gardini and Mondt had wrestled for an hour in an even match. Gardini grabbed a headlock, but Mondt slipped out. Gardini transitioned into a crotch hold and slammed Mondt to the mat. Gardini won the first fall in 1 hour, six minutes.[cli]

Mondt hit the mat hard and appeared woozy. The ringside physician checked on Mondt based on his actions. The doctor told the referee Mondt couldn't continue the match.[clii] The referee awarded Gardini the second fall and match due to Mondt's injury.

Mondt used the injury angle for the final time in 1922 during a November 14th match with Dick Daviscourt. By this time, Mondt had joined with Sandow and Lewis. Mondt lost a 2-out-of-3 falls match to Ed "Strangler" Lewis on November 10, 1922.[cliii]

The match with Daviscourt was again 2-out-of-3 falls but this time the match wouldn't end after the first fall. Mondt won the first fall with a Japanese step over.[cliv]

Daviscourt won the second fall with a slam, which brought the injury angle into play. Mondt again struck the mat hard causing the ringside doctor to recommend the referee end the match. The doctor thought Mondt suffered a spinal injury.[clv]

Mondt continued to exhibit and develop his promotional ability. However, his greatest contribution to the Gold Dust Trio was as Lewis' sparring partner.

Burns knew Mondt could keep Lewis sharp in case an opponent decided to try a double-cross. Burns' initial recommendation to Sandow was based on Mondt's hooking ability. Mondt's training with Lewis would also take Mondt's own skills to a new level.

Mondt's ability would also be of great value in dispatching bothersome challenges from wrestlers wanting to have a contest with Lewis. Mondt would serve as the policeman, who you would have to defeat to challenge Lewis.

Although it would mean different things later, in this era a policeman was a skilled shooter, or preferably hooker, who the champion had already beaten in worked matches. The champion would question the challenger's credentials to wrestle him for the title.

To prove his worthiness, the challenger would have to wrestle the policeman, in this case Mondt, to prove his worthiness. Mondt's goal in the match was to beat, and hopefully injure, the challenger. If he defeated the challenger, the fans and pundits would not see the challenger as serious anymore since Lewis had beaten Mondt several times in the past.

If the challenger won but his opponent injured him, he would be easy pickings for the champion in the match. However, there is not much evidence of any challenges with Lewis as champion and Mondt as policeman.

With a lack of legitimate challenges, Sandow, Lewis and Mondt were free to concentrate on the promotional and money-making side of professional wrestling. Burns original recommendation letter to Sandow proved true.

"He's a big kid but he knows the game. He's as good a wrestler as you will find…He's got a good head on him too, and if you give him a chance he'll develop, not only into a great wrestler, but he'll be a help to you in the business."[clvi]

"Toots" Mondt joining with Sandow, and Lewis created the most dominant combination in American professional wrestling at the time. The Gold Dust Trio dominated professional wrestling for the next five to six years.

Figure 30-Joseph "Toots" Mondt from the Public Domain

Chapter 9 – The Trio Changes Wrestling

By controlling the World Championship, the Gold Dust Trio updated the wrestling business in style of wrestling, card make-up and wrestlers used by promoters. The Trio instituted changes, which would affect wrestling long after others took over management and promotion.

One of the sources used for this chapter is *Fall Guys: The Barnums of Bounce* by Marcus Griffin. Griffin, although a reporter, worked for the Buffalo promotional office in the 1930s.

After the Buffalo Office fired him, he used his insider's knowledge to expose the business as revenge for his firing.[clvii] Griffin's book is problematic for a couple reasons.

First, he was in the office in the 1930s, but his book goes back to the time of Frank Gotch in the first decade of the 20th Century. Griffin relied on hearsay information from insiders, but it wasn't always accurate. Griffin may have misinterpreted or misremembered some of the information. He may also have been the victim of wrestlers' propensity for store telling.

The second problem is his revenge motive. He authored the book to expose the worked nature of professional wrestling to hurt the promoters, who fired him. Griffin took some literary license with the truth to make wrestling look worse.

As an example of factual error, he states Mondt joined the Gold Dust Trio around 1920 but Mondt wasn't with them until 1922.[clviii] He also stated Lewis had a grudge against Curley over the 1915 New York International Wrestling Tournament.

According to Griffin, Lewis beat everyone, but Curley denied him the tournament title. However, Sam Rachmann was the promoter for the tournaments, which occurred in the spring and fall.

Curley was only co-promoter of the fall version.

Lewis also didn't beat everyone. He lost, like everyone else, to the tournament champion Aleksander "Alex" Aberg. The tournament competitors wrestled the matches by Greco-Roman wrestling rules. Aberg beat everyone in this style. Lewis also only drew with Wladek Zbyszko in the Greco-Roman match.[clix] Aberg refused to wrestle Lewis in a catch-as-catch-can match although Wladek Zbyszko did wrestle Lewis in this style during the fall tournament.

With these caveats stated upfront, the book does contain a lot of behind-the-scenes information on how the Gold Dust Trio operated during their zenith. When possible, I use other sources to cross-check information.

Mondt's first contribution to the workings of the Trio was to change the style of wrestling. Because wrestling had consisted of a mix of actual contests and worked matches prior to 1915, the style of wrestling seen in legitimate matches still dominated.

The problem was legitimate contests could often be very long and boring with little action. Both wrestlers feared making a mistake, so the matches were often stale mates. Imagine seeing two wrestlers in a collar-and-elbow tie-up for two to four hours. Not an exciting spectator sport.

Since wrestlers worked matches now, unless it was a double-cross, or rare agreed upon contests, Mondt wanted to add more exciting sequences and make matches shorter. The Trio did not make the change all at once but over the next several years. The chaining of wrestling holds together became more common.

Mondt also shortened the matches. Matches under the main event would normally finish in under 30 minutes. The main event would still be an hour or two.

The shorter matches also led to cards moving from 1 to 2 matches to 3 to 4 matches. While paying more wrestlers

136

per card would seem to be a bad idea, the added wrestlers often added interest. If a card was only two matches and fans weren't interested in any of the four, it was hard to draw a house. Adding a few wrestlers increased the chances of drawing fan interest in one of the other wrestlers under the main event.

Crowds continued to grow, and the Trio made more profits per show despite paying more wrestlers. Business was so good that Ed "Strangler" Lewis was the highest paid professional athlete of the 1920s.

Mondt convinced Sandow of one more change, which would make them lots of money but lots of enemies. Mondt convinced Sandow to book wrestling like vaudeville booked its shows.[clx] In effect, they created an early booking office.

Sandow had one headache, when it came to booking Lewis as World Champion, the disorganized nature of American professional wrestling. In some cities, like New York and Boston, you had well established promoters Jack Curley and Paul Bowser, respectively. They employed their own local wrestlers and had a challenger built up locally for the World Champion.

Other promoters didn't employ local wrestlers often, so Sandow had to supply both the champion and a challenger. Sandow could often book wrestler traveling the circuit like Lewis. However, this practice could also create problems.

Griffin used a specific example in chapter 5 of Fall Guys. If Sandow booked a wrestler with a strong local or even national reputation to wrestle in Lewis in Kansas City later in September, the wrestler would also look for bookings in nearby cities.

If the wrestler booked himself in St. Louis in early September but lost the match, the newspapers in Kansas City would normally pick up this news from St. Louis. The Kansas City card would then

struggle to be profitable because Lewis'
challenger had recently lost in the
area.clxi

Mondt had an idea to address these
situations based on his time with
"Farmer" Burns. Well into his fifties,
Burns was still training wrestlers and
traveling around the country.

When Frank Gotch was World Champion,
Burns was his manager and trainer. Burns
also trained several up-and-coming
wrestlers, who traveled with Burns and
Gotch.

When Gotch went to a town with an
established promoter and developed local
challenger, Gotch defended his title in
the main event. Burns' other wrestlers
were usually not on the card.

However, if a promoter booked Gotch
without an established local pool of
talent, Burns' other wrestlers would fill
out the one or two match undercard. One
of his wrestlers, often Burns himself,
would then wrestle Gotch in a worked
match "for the World Title." Burns and

the promoter would then split the profits based on predetermined split.

Had the Trio used such a booking scheme, everyone would have gone along with it. Future booking offices would operate exactly this way. However, Mondt had a unique twist on Burns' scheme.

In vaudeville, each circuit had a developed number of acts. They would book their shows into local theaters, but local talent would not perform on the shows. The Trio only allowed contracted performers for the circuit to wrestle.

The vaudeville circuit dictated the split to local theaters. If they didn't like the split, they could look for another vaudeville company or not run a show.

Sandow and Mondt decided that Lewis would only wrestle on cards comprised of wrestlers signed with Sandow. Even promoters like Curley and Bowser could only use the Trio's talent not their local talent on shows with Lewis.

The Trio established a 50-50 gate split. The Trio would get 50 percent of the gate, which Sandow used to pay the wrestlers. The remainder was their profit. The promoter would use his 50 percent for overhead and advertising. The remainder was his profit.

The split led to far smaller profits for promoters like Curley and Bowser, who previously only had to pay a booking fee for the champion (often 10% of the gate). It also made it unprofitable for them to develop local wrestlers as they would not be able to book them to wrestle the champion.

Further inflaming the situation was Sandow's planting friendly promoters like Tom Law in undeveloped Midwestern cities to start promotions. While Curley and Bowser promoted the big cities and exercised tremendous power in American professional wrestling, they now found themselves treated like any other promoter. The situation didn't sit well with either promoter.

This controversial decision to only book their wrestlers on a Lewis' show eventually blew-up in the Gold Dust Trio's faces but from 1922 to 1925, it was a license to print money. Sandow, Lewis and Mondt made a fortune over the next few years.

Figure 31-"Strangler" Lewis in the 1910s (Public Domain)

Chapter 10 – Lewis Defends the Championship

While Sandow and Mondt began to consolidate the business side of American professional wrestling, Lewis set about defending his world championship. Even without Sandow and Mondt making enemies left and right, Lewis would still have to be vigilant for double-crosses.

Few wrestlers had a chance of beating Lewis but Stanislaus Zbyszko, Joe Stecher or John "Tigerman" Pesek might try. Lewis also had to be aware of the referee. Titles could change hands on a disqualification during this era. The referee could be critical in a successful double-cross particularly when the opponent cannot beat the champion in a legitimate contest.

The talk leading into 1923 was a potential boxer versus wrestler match between Lewis and Jack Dempsey. The chatter around the match was getting louder and fans were anticipating a combat sports spectacle. Once again, sports journalist Frank G. Menke would spoil the hype.[clxii]

Menke first took issue with the proposed location for the match, Wichita, Kansas. While Wichita was a large wrestling town, promoters would book a Dempsey-Lewis mixed bout in New York City or Chicago.

Menke also pointed out that Jack Kearns, Dempsey's manager, was too wise to risk his fighter in a difficult matchup with a wrestler. Menke pointed out that wrestlers win these matches. If the boxer cannot knock out the wrestler, when the wrestler goes for the clinch, the boxer ends up on the mat. On the ground, the boxer is helpless favoring the wrestler.[clxiii]

Menke explained both managers went along with the potential bout because the publicity benefitted both Lewis and Dempsey. They continued to express interest in a match they never intended to have to capitalize on the publicity. Menke was right again as the bout never materialized.

An interesting photo appeared in the *Perth Amboy Evening News* in February 1923. The photo showed future movie stuntman and current champion steer wrestler Yakima Canutt demonstrating Canutt's headlock on a steer.[clxiv] Lewis was supposed to be getting pointers for his headlock applications. Lewis was a mainstream pop culture icon in the 1920s.

SHOWING ED LEWIS IN ACTION

"Strangler" Lewis, wrestling champ, picking up a few pointers from Yakima Canutt, champion steer wrestler and broncho rider of Colorado. The hold shown is known as a headlock.

Figure 32-Photo of Lewis and Canutt (Public Domain)

Jack Curley promoted Nat "Panther" Pendleton, the future movie star, as a potential challenger to Lewis. After a controversial decision that many observers felt cost Pendleton the Olympic

Gold Medal in wrestling, the former collegiate champion began wrestling professionally.

Figure 33-Nat Pendleton Wrestling (Public Domain)

Jack Curley backed Pendleton's challenge, but an agreed upon contest with John "Tigerman" Pesek derailed Curley's plan. Pesek injured Pendleton, who eventually transitioned to acting in films. Pesek soon popped up on Lewis' radar.

A skilled submission wrestler, Pesek was the ideal hooker to have contests with "trust busters" Marin Plestina and Nat Pendleton. Booking Pesek to wrestle your champion was a bit dicey. If Pesek decided to turn the exhibition into a contest, he was capable of legitimately defeating most wrestlers.

Lewis was the top of the food chain, when it came to skilled hookers, but Pesek might have been close. Lewis would be aware of a potential double-cross with Pesek.

Pesek had been on quite a winning streak in Kansas City, Missouri going into his May 2, 1923, match with Lewis. The newspaper coverage did not include attendance figures for this match, but Lewis drew well in Kansas City. Lewis and Pesek could have easily drawn 8,000 to 10,000 fans.

While Lewis and Pesek normally cooperated with each other in matches, it was obvious Lewis wouldn't expose himself to a bad position. After an hour of pushing each other around the ring, Lewis finally got Pesek to the mat. Pesek quickly submitted to the toehold at the 1 hour, 2-minute mark.[clxv]

Lewis secured a second toehold for the second fall and match at 2 minutes, 30 seconds. Lewis won the match in two straight falls. The quick second fall reveals it to be a work, but Lewis obviously didn't trust Pesek. He didn't attempt a headlock in the entire match.

The loss hurt Pesek as the newspaper coverage of his performance was very negative. The reporters said Pesek would have to leave Kansas City to rebuild his reputation because the loss seriously harmed his ability to draw a crowd in Kansas City.[clxvi]

Lewis was right to be careful with Pesek. Pesek worked the first two falls of a match with disputed World Champion

Joe Stecher in 1926. During the third fall, Pesek shot on Stecher by catching him in a double arm wristlock. Pesek forced Stecher to submit but the referee controversially disqualified Pesek. Fans did not like it, but the referee's decision stood.[clxvii]

Stecher had beaten Pesek in a contest in 1920 but the men had also worked a few matches including two earlier in 1926. Considering Pesek a friend, Stecher didn't take precautions with him and almost lost his title.

Prior to Pesek wrestling Lewis, the first signs of a rising resentment to the Gold Dust Trio emerged. Sandow booked Lewis for a match with regular opponent Cliff Binckley instead of Jack Curley's preferred opponent, Wladek Zbyszko.[clxviii]

The New York Athletic Commission stepped in and declared Sandow must bill the Lewis-Binckley match as an exhibition instead of a contest. The commission reasoned that Lewis had beaten Binckley all over the country.[clxix] They didn't say the men worked the matches, which they did, but instead stated Binckley did not represent a legitimate threat to Lewis' title.

Figure 34-Wladek Zbyszko in the 1910s

The commissions' actions prevented betting, which could be another lucrative revenue stream for the Gold Dust Trio. Curley had enough political influence to prevent the switch to an exhibition if he wanted to. Curley's refusal to act revealed the strain in Curley and Sandow's former partnership.

This situation was also unique because this time the champion was the irritant not Sandow's and Mondt's business practice. Lewis was not a hot head and usually maintained good relations with the other wrestlers. Even when he wrestled other wrestlers legitimately, he didn't hurt them with his submissions when he easily could.

However, Lewis had two mat rivals, who both got under his skin for different reasons. The result was the same for both men though. Lewis refused to grant them a world title match during this second title reign from 1922 to 1925. Lewis' refusal to wrestle the men cost them their best pay days of the year. As a rule, world title matches drew the biggest gates.

Lewis first wrestled with Wladek Zbyszko in 1914. The 22-year-olds met in Detroit, Michigan in a rough contest, which lasted about 20 minutes before Lewis tired of Zbyszko's tactics. Lewis punched Zbyszko with a strong right hand, a clear disqualification.

Zbyszko was groggy for a second. After clearing his head, Zbyszko punched Lewis back. Both men began pummeling each other as the referee struggled to separate them.

A large part of the crowd was Polish and took exception to Lewis striking Zbyszko. The fans began to push towards the ring. It took a large squad of Detroit Police to repel the crowd.

Despite the bad blood, both men wrestled contests in the 1915 New York International Tournament without any issues. Zbyszko won the Greco-Roman wrestling matches, while Lewis won the catch-as-catch-can matches.

In the late 1910s, the men worked several matches together including exchanging the American Heavyweight Wrestling Championship. The cooperation ended in the early 1920s.

According to Marcus Griffin, Wladek Zbyszko created new animosity, when he tried to double-cross and hook Lewis in a worked match. Instead, Lewis broke Zbyszko's arm.[clxx]

I've never been able to find another source on the Rochester, New York match, where this incident was supposed to occur. Wladek Zbyszko would have been crazy to try to hook Lewis, a much better submission wrestler but I can't say it didn't happen.

Lewis told Lou Thesz that both Zbyszko brothers had a tell, when they were thinking about shooting on an opponent.[clxxi] Obviously, for Lewis to pick up on the tell, both brothers must have thought about shooting on him during a match.

Whether it stemmed from some version of the incident reported in *The Fall Guys* or just personal dislike, Lewis wouldn't wrestle Wladek Zbyszko particularly after Jack Curley started backing the younger Zbyszko.

Lewis didn't have any problems with Stanislaus Zbyszko with whom he continued to work matches. On May 22, 1923, Lewis defeated Zbyszko in a one fall match in Minneapolis, Minnesota. Lewis won the fall with the headlock.[clxxii]

Stanislaus Zbyszko remained on good terms with the Gold Dust Trio throughout the next three years. If he resented the treatment of his younger brother, who he was close to and lived with for several years after returning to the United States, he hid it well.

Lewis' longest standing professional rivalry was with Joe Stecher. This long-held animosity kept Joe iced out of championship matches also. As I stated earlier in this book, Stecher was the superior wrestler earlier in their careers but eventually Lewis surpassed Stecher.

Even though both men took part in primarily worked matches, they struggled to cooperate with each other. Stecher dropped his title to Lewis in a worked match in 1920. However, many of their matches were contests. Neither seemed willing or able to work with the other man for long.

The Stechers became desperate enough to offer $15,000 to Lewis to secure a title match.[clxxiii] Paul Bowser also decided to align with the Stechers. He hoped to secure a contest with Lewis, but Lewis continued to ignore the brothers and their new ally.

In late 1923, Lewis created news of a different kind by divorcing his wife, Dr. Ada Scott Morton Fredericks. (Robert Friedrich was Lewis actual name. It was often written up in newspapers as Fredericks.) His wife was surprised as she believed they were still on good terms.

Lewis was leaving Dr. Fredericks, who built him a $5,000 gymnasium on her San Jose estate, for a Russian princess he met on a tour of Germany in 1921.[clxxiv] Lewis was not a faithful husband to any of his reported five wives. Lewis and Dr. Fredericks had a two-year-old daughter, who would be staying with her mother.

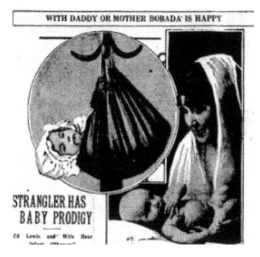

WITH DADDY OR MOTHER BOBADA' IS HAPPY

STRANGLER HAS BABY PRODIGY

Figure 35-Photo of Ada Scott Morton Lewis and baby from the May 12, 1921, the Bismarck Tribune (Public Domain)

Other than the Pesek match, Lewis had an uneventful but highly profitable 1923. Lewis wrestled several matches with Stanislaus Zbyszko but few other big names. "Toots" Mondt was also a frequent opponent.

Lewis usually went home to San Jose, California for the Christmas and New Year holidays. He would then start wrestling again in the middle of January.

Lewis began his 1924 campaign by wrestling Judo black belt Taro Miyaki in a mixed match. Lewis threw Miyaki twice with the headlock in a little over 20 minutes.[clxxv]

Lewis' next big match was in Chicago at the end of February. Lewis would face old foe Stanislaus Zbyszko. The match became very real for Lewis at the end of the third fall.

Lewis and Zbyszko worked the match along the same formula as past matches. Lewis took the first fall with a headlock at 24 minutes, 45 seconds. Zbyszko won the second fall in 7 minutes, 30 seconds with a short arm scissors.[clxxvi]

During the third fall, in a spot worked out by Lewis and Zbyszko to make the third fall controversial, Lewis appeared to poke Zbyszko in the eyes. After such an obvious foul, Zbyszko grabbed a headlock and won the third fall at 11 minutes.[clxxvii]

Because Chicago crowds had never previously supported a foreign-born wrestler over an American-born wrestler, the police were not on high alert at the finish of the match. However, dozens of fans rushed the ring with the intention of attacking Lewis and the referee. Promoter Jack Coffey and a large group of police officers and firefighters, assisting with security, rushed the ring to save Lewis and the referee.[clxxviii]

Furious crowds presented the real danger for Lewis in his second title reign. Other wrestlers didn't pose near the danger angry crowds did for the champion.

One of Lewis' frequent opponents in 1924 was his training and business partner, "Toots" Mondt. They wrestled each other in Rochester, New York in early May.

In a sequence worked out by Mondt, Lewis appeared dazed and confused by the ropes at the 1 hour, 37-minute mark. Mondt sportingly backed off to allow Lewis to recover when Lewis jumped to his feet. Lewis ran into Mondt from behind. Mondt fell awkwardly to the mat allowing Lewis to gain a quick pin fall.[clxxix]

The fans, who were clearly behind Mondt, saw Lewis' "cheap trick" and reacted violently. Only a squad of police officers prevented the fans from attacking Lewis. The match was supposed to be two-out-of-three falls, but the unruly crowd halted the match after the first fall.[clxxx]

Outside the ring, Lewis found himself in legal trouble on August 11, 1924. Returning from Tijuana with a party of friends, Lewis engaged in a vehicle accident right inside the U.S. border. Mrs. Daisy Haynes of San Diego, the driver of the vehicle, which Lewis struck, was upset about the accident. She heatedly asked Lewis to look at the damage.[clxxxi]

Lewis refused. Her son, obviously not aware of who "Strangler" Lewis was, took offense and challenged Lewis. A few punches later, Mrs. Haynes' son was on the ground. Fortunately for him, Lewis only punched him instead of putting him in a submission.

Lewis and his party left the area, but the Sheriff arrested Lewis 35 miles later. Prosecutors charged Lewis with four counts of assault and one charge of disturbing the peace.[clxxxii] Lewis would not suffer any serious repercussions from this incident though.

Lewis also had a new wife, the former Bessie McNear.[clxxxiii] Lewis' relationship with the Russian princess must have been a whirlwind marriage and divorce.

Lewis finished out the year with matches against familiar opponents "Toots" Mondt, Renato Gardini and Dick Daviscourt.

By this point, Lewis had held the World Championship for over two and a half years. To prevent an erosion in fan interest, Sandow decided they needed to create a new star and title challenger. Sandow had set his eyes on a prospect from another sport. Sandow started building him up in 1924 with the plan of having Lewis wrestle him in 1925. This fateful decision would lead to dire consequences for the Gold Dust Trio and their dominance of professional wrestling.

TO HAVE AND TO HOLD—ED. LEWIS HOLDS

San Francisco—Introducing Ed "Strangler" Lewis, heavy
weight wrestler champ of the world, demonstrating his famous
and deadly headlock to his bride, the former Bessie McNear.
Half Nelsons and headlocks mean nothing to Mrs. Lewis now.
They're all loving caresses with new names.

Figure 36-"Strangler" Lewis and his third wife Bessie McNear (Public Domain)

Chapter 11 – An Unlikely Choice

Sandow's unlikely choice for title challenger was a former collegiate football player from Nebraska. "Big" Wayne Munn stood around 6'05" to 6'06". His weight fluctuated between 230 and 260 pounds. Munn's exceptional size and strength were his top athletic selling point.

Sandow saw newspaper photos of Munn and Munn's physical presence arrested Sandow's attention. Sandow saw immense drawing power in Munn's unique physical appearance. In late 1923, he began to recruit Munn with the intention of making him a top star.

Lewis and Mondt were not as enthusiastic as Sandow for one reason. Munn had no wrestling experience. They could train him for the ring, but he would never be more than a performer. It would take years to turn Munn into a world class shooter or hooker.

Figure 37-"Big" Wayne Munn from the Public Domain

Always worried about double-crosses, Lewis and Mondt told Sandow it would be a bad idea to push Munn too hard.

Almost any legitimate wrestler could shoot on Munn and expose him as a fraud.

Sandow reassured Lewis and Mondt that he would only let Munn get into the ring with wrestlers financially dependent or loyal to the Gold Dust Trio. With these assurances, Lewis and Mondt reluctantly began training Munn for the ring.

Munn had his first match on March 4, 1924. Munn wrestled Jack Paulsen in the preliminary match on the Lewis-Taro Miyaki card in Kansas City, Missouri. Munn threw Paulsen in two straight falls. Munn ended both falls with the headlock in 5 minutes, 10 seconds and 4 minutes, 10 seconds, respectively.[clxxxiv]

Mondt wrestled in the other match on the three-match card. Lewis and Mondt were keeping a protective eye on Munn.

They were also keeping his matches short to put him over strong and to hide his inexperience as he learned how to work wrestling matches. On March 25th, Munn wrestled Joe Zongalewicz on the undercard of a Lewis-Stanislaus Zbyszko match. Munn won the match with a headlock in 2 minutes, 30 seconds.[clxxxv]

With his collegiate background and growing popularity in the professional ranks, several colleges offered Munn a job coaching wrestling.[clxxxvi] Munn wisely turned down the offers, which would have exposed his lack of wrestling knowledge.

Munn scored his biggest victory in Kansas City, Missouri on June 4, 1924. Munn defeated former American Heavyweight Wrestling Champion Charley Cutler in two straight falls.[clxxxvii] He won the first fall in 5 minutes, 20 seconds. Munn scored the second fall in only 1 minute, 40 seconds.

For most of the remainder of 1924, Munn wrestled in Kansas City, while preparing for the match with "Strangler" Lewis. Lewis and "Toots" Mondt were his main training partners.

Figure 38-Wayne "Big" Munn circa 1925 (Public Domain)

Despite their training, Munn hadn't developed any ability to wrestle. He could only work matches, most of which the Trio kept very short. Once more, they tried to talk Sandow out of putting the championship on him.

Sandow could only see the money from the full houses he believed Munn would draw. He told his partner to trust him. He would protect Munn. Again, Lewis and Mondt agreed but Sandow had sown the seeds of dissension, particularly with Mondt.

To build their future title match, Lewis started putting over Munn as a potential challenger in the press. While Lewis stated the obvious, Munn was not the wrestler Lewis was, he said Munn's size and strength would make him a tough challenge for any wrestler.[clxxxviii]

On Friday, October 24, 1924, the wrestling season kicked off in Kansas City, Missouri at the Convention Hall. Before air conditioning in buildings, wrestling was only a fall, winter, and spring sport in some areas. With the humid Missouri summers, it was the case in Kansas City.

5,000 fans showed up for the first night of wrestling with Wayne "Big" Munn headlining the card. Munn wrestled Alex Lundin. Sandow billed Munn at 250 pounds, while billing Lundin at 235 pounds. Ringside reporters thought Munn looked much bigger than Lundin though.[clxxxix]

Munn grabbed Lundin with a crotch and body hold and dumped him for the first fall in only 3 minutes, 32 seconds. Munn repeated the feat with the same hold for the second fall. It took him 3 seconds longer to secure the second fall.[cxc]

On Wednesday, November 19, 1924, Munn met part-time wrestler and Canadian Mountie Wallace Dugid. Munn was using the crotch and body hold a lot as he won the first fall in 11 minutes, 30 seconds.[cxci]

Munn secured the second fall with the same hold in 2 minutes, one second.[cxcii] It made sense for Munn to use this hold as it emphasized his power and strength.

Switching to the crotch hold was a great move for Munn's development. Previously, he used the headlock, but you wouldn't want a match between Lewis and Munn using the same hold over and over. The crotch hold could also highlight Munn's strength in picking up large opponents.

Munn had shown his dominance in short matches but to be the champion, he would have to be able to perform in longer matches. "Toots" Mondt decided to book himself with Munn to carry Munn in his first long match. This match was also the setup for the Lewis-Munn match as Sandow promised the winner a title shot with "Strangler" Lewis.

Munn and Mondt met on Thursday, December 11, 1924, at the Convention Hall in Kansas City. They were the second match on the card as the main event was Lewis defending his title versus Hasson Giles.

Munn continued to look dominant in his matches as he threw Mondt around the ring. Mondt's offense consisted primarily of fouling Munn. Munn was being setup as the baby face challenger. Lewis would be the heel in their title match.

It took Munn 29 minutes, 35 seconds, to win the first fall from Mondt by far Munn's longest match to date. Mondt saw what he needed because the second fall only took 4 minutes, 20 seconds for Munn to again throw Mondt with the crotch hold.[cxciii]

Lewis won his match in two straight falls as well. Promoters announced the Lewis-Munn title match for January 8, 1925, in Kansas City, Missouri. It was Lewis' last scheduled title defense before he left for a tour of Europe.

Despite the unpredictability of winter weather in Missouri, the January title bout went on as scheduled. The build up to the match had been perfect as 10,000 fans crowded Convention Hall to see the anticipated title match.[cxciv]

Although the crowd clearly favored Munn, all the smart money was on Lewis retaining his title. Knowledgeable fans and reporters believed Munn was too inexperienced to beat the dominant champion.

Munn surprised everyone by starting the match on the offensive. Munn picked up Lewis repeatedly with the crotch hold, stood with Lewis to demonstrate his strength and then Munn slammed Lewis to the mat.[cxcv] Several times, Lewis struck his head on the mat.

Lewis tried to secure the headlock several times but failed to get the grip on Munn's head. Munn pushed Lewis forward only for Lewis to spin back around to Munn. Munn would then pick Lewis up and slam him to the mat.

Munn slammed Lewis hard at the 21-minute mark and followed him to the mat. Munn pinned Lewis for the first fall. It took Lewis five minutes to get back to his feet. Lewis' seconds helped support him as he struggled to the back for the first intermission.[cxcvi]

The controversy in the match occurred during the second fall. Lewis had just missed a headlock by the ropes when Munn picked Lewis up with the crotch hold. At this point, Lewis ended up outside the ring, where he hit the floor hard.

Munn told referee Walter Bates that Lewis was wriggling out of the crotch hold, which caused Lewis to fall over the ropes. Lewis was insensible on the floor, but his manager claimed Munn purposely threw Lewis to the floor. He wanted Munn disqualified and the match awarded to Lewis.[cxcvii]

Bates did disqualify Munn for the second fall. The men now each had a fall apiece. However, he refused to end the match. Bates told Sandow that Lewis had 15 minutes to recover or forfeit the match.[cxcviii]

Lewis' seconds helped him from ringside. He did return to the ring after

20 minutes but still appeared dazed. Due to Lewis weakened condition, Munn won the third fall, match, and title in only 50 seconds with the crotch hold and slam. The fans went crazy as Munn celebrated his championship win.[cxcix]

Ed "Strangler" Lewis, despite his misgivings, dropped the title to Munn. With the enthusiastic response to Munn, Sandow was convinced that putting the belt on Munn was the best move for their business. However, Sandow would have to carefully manage Munn.

First, Munn did not possess any real wrestling skills. Munn would be extremely vulnerable to any moderately skilled wrestler, who wanted to shoot on Munn and legitimately take the title.

Second, Lewis was heading off for a tour of Europe. Wrestlers would think twice about shooting on Munn with Lewis and Mondt in the building. Without this protection, Munn was even more exposed to double-crosses.

Sandow decided to turn to a former World Champion, who he trusted. Since Lewis was unavailable for a few months, Munn could cement his reputation as the new top star and build legitimacy for his title reign by beating another contender. Sandow believed this wrestler was the perfect choice.

NEW WRESTLING CHAMPION

Wayne (Big) Munn, who ripped the heavyweight wrestling crown off Ed Lewis' dome last night at Kansas City, is the tallest man in the mat game. The former Nebraska football star used his height and bulk to advantage in shaking off Lewis' attempts to clamp on a headlock and flipped the "Strangler" over the the ropes, a performance that brought cheers from the 17,000 excited fans that watched the match.

Figure 39-"Big" Wayne Munn demonstrating his size compared to normal sized men (Public Domain)

Chapter 12 – The Grand Old Man Back in the Title Picture

With Lewis unavailable on a European Tour, Sandow chose Stanislaus Zbyszko to wrestle Wayne Munn in his early title defenses. Sandow felt Zbyszko's reputation would build Munn as a legitimate champion. Most importantly, Sandow trusted Zbyszko.

Stanislaus Zbyszko had remained in good graces with the Gold Dust Trio. When it came time for Zbyszko to drop the title back to Lewis, he did so without issue. He and Lewis worked several rematches over the next two years. The Grand Old Man of Wrestling was Lewis' most credible challenger during his second reign.

Even though Lewis refused to wrestle Wladek Zbyszko, Sandow and Lewis seemed to like and respect Stanislaus Zbyszko. Sandow approached Zbyszko about wrestling Munn. Zbyszko reassured Sandow he would be happy to help get the young champion established.

Zbyszko was approaching 45 years of age and knew his wrestling career was winding down. Since they had billed him as 5 years older than he was, fans thought he was 50 years old. It was getting harder to convince fans to pay to see an older wrestler, who they viewed as past his prime. Few, if any, people outside of wrestling knew Zbyszko could still legitimately beat most of the professional wrestlers of the time.

Since losing the title back to "Strangler" Lewis, Zbyszko had been inactive. Other than high profile rematches with Lewis, Zbyszko had only wrestled John Pesek, Joe Stecher and Jim Londos. Although he looked strong in all three matches, Zbyszko lost the matches with all three men. Zbyszko was becoming the king maker for future wrestling stars.

Sandow thought Zbyszko could do the same with Wayne Munn. It was a mistake, which would cost him dearly.

Figure 40-Stanislaus Zbyszko circa 1919 (Public Domain)

Chapter 13 – The Double-Cross

Sandow wasted no time matching Munn with Zbyszko. Munn would make his first title defense against Zbyszko at Kansas City's Convention Hall on Wednesday, February 11, 1925.

Munn's first title defense drew another capacity crowd of 10,000 fans.[cc] Munn's early title reign was proving Sandow's belief in Munn's ability to have a lucrative run with the championship. Munn's strength was his ability to draw fans to the matches. Munn still didn't possess much actual wrestling skill though.

The crowd cheered wildly for Munn although the jeering for Zbyszko was more muted than for Lewis. The fans did not have much animosity towards "The Grand Old Man."

Zbyszko avoided many of Munn's attempts to catch him with the crotch hold. The *Kansas City Times* reporter noted that Zbyszko made a better showing in this match than Lewis did, when he lost the title a month earlier.[cci]

However, Munn caught Zbyszko with the crotch hold at about the 16-minute mark and dumped Zbyszko to the mat. Zbyszko tried to squirm free, but Munn applied a half-Nelson to turn Zbyszko onto his back. Referee Walter Bates, the same referee from the Munn-Lewis bout, awarded Munn the first fall.[ccii]

Zbyszko did not appear tired or injured to start the second fall, so Munn would have his work cut out for him. Munn would remain on the offensive, while Zbyszko primarily wrestled defensively not venturing to attack Munn.

Munn tried to gain a headlock, but Zbyszko shrugged him off as he did to Lewis so many times. Munn next went for a scissors hold and arm bar. Zbyszko again powered out of the attempt.[cciii] Zbyszko seemed more of a match for Munn in the power department than Munn's previous opponents.

Finally, Munn grabbed a second crotch hold and repeated the same sequence from the first fall. After turning Zbyszko onto his back with the half-Nelson, Bates awarded Munn the match in two straight falls.[cciv] The second fall took a little over 12 minutes.

Zbyszko made Munn look strong in his first title defense without any incidents. Sandow must have felt good about his strategy of matching Munn with Zbyszko after this match.

Happy with this result, Sandow booked a rematch between Munn and Zbyszko in Philadelphia in early April 1925. Sandow was looking forward to another strong victory to further cement Munn's status as World Champion.

On March 6th, Munn was in Cleveland, Ohio to defend his title against Canadian champion Wallace Dugid. Munn again won in two straight falls but this time in under 12 minutes for both falls.[ccv] "Strangler" Lewis also wrestled on this card, so he was back from his European tour already.

Figure 41-Wayne Munn and Stanislaus Zbyszko from the April 16, 1925, Pittsburgh Post-Gazette (Public Domain)

On April 15, 1925, Munn defended his title against Stanislaus Zbyszko for the second time. Zbyszko wrestled very differently this time around. Philadelphia was the perfect setting for a double-cross.

As events unfolded, none of the Gold Dust Trio was in Philadelphia that night. Sandow's brother, Max Baumann, was managing John Pesek, who wrestled earlier on the card.[ccvi] Max was likely in charge that night and responsible for the card.

The match drew 8,000 fans to the Philadelphia Arena. Munn and Zbyszko met at center ring for the customary handshake and the match began.

Unlike previous matches, Munn and Zbyszko tied up in the collar and elbow position and stayed there for several minutes. Zbyszko kept his legs far behind him to prevent Munn from grabbing his crotch hold.

After several minutes of pushing and batting each other, Zbyszko executed a switch, spun to Munn's back and lifted the 265-pounder off the mat. Zbyszko slammed Munn onto his hands and knees.[ccvii]

Max Baumann must have gotten concerned as the plan was for Zbyszko to put Munn over strong in this rematch. It must have slowly begun to dawn on him that Zbyszko was not going along with the agreed upon finish.

Zbyszko removed all doubt, when he used a forearm hold into cross-body hold to pin Munn at 8 minutes, 11 seconds.[ccviii] Munn caught on quicker than Baumann as the *Philadelphia Inquirer* reporter stated Munn had a shocked look on his face from the 3-minute mark of the first fall on.

Munn returned to his dressing room for the 10-minute intermission, but Stanislaus Zbyszko remained in the ring. Max Baumann came out to the ring and attempted to talk to Zbyszko.[ccix] Zbyszko sat impassively and refused to engage with Baumann.

Others also tried to talk to Zbyszko, who sat with his mouth tightly closed and only shook his head "no" as he looked at the mat. Zbyszko was committed to his course of action.

According to the version the Gold Dust Trio circulated later, the men were trying to convince Zbyszko to reschedule the match with Champion Munn, who was running a 104-degree fever. However, the ringside physician undercut the sick champion argument. Dr. Baron said Munn had tonsillitis but didn't have a fever nor appear sick.[ccx] Munn passed the pre-match physical.

Munn finally returned to the ring. Zbyszko quickly finished off Munn for the second fall. Zbyszko again took Munn's back, slammed him to the mat and turned Munn onto his back with a forearm hold and hammerlock. At 4 minutes, 53 seconds, Zbyszko won the second fall, match, and championship.[ccxi]

The fans cheered wildly as a group of Philadelphia police officers escorted Zbyszko to the dressing room. Zbyszko waited a full 15 minutes before he let reporters in to speak with him. The squad of police officers then escorted him to his hotel, where police protected him until he left town.[ccxii] Zbyszko and his co-conspirators, the Stecher brothers, Jack Curley, and Paul Bowser, were concerned someone would attempt to kill Zbyszko.

Before Zbyszko left Philadelphia, the newspapers were already reporting on a potential May match between Lewis and Zbyszko in Michigan. However, the Stecher group had different ideas. They didn't go through so much trouble in executing the double-cross to give Lewis a chance to win the title back.

The plotters congratulated themselves and smiles were plentiful. They couldn't see what the negative consequences of their actions would be. The double-cross would hurt everyone financially over the next few years. Fans were confused by the resulting matches and machinations of the Gold Dust Trio and their enemies. The double-cross also ended two wrestling careers, a short, brilliant one and a legendary one.

Figure 42-Stanislaus Zbyszko When He Still Had Hair (Public Domain)

Chapter 14 – Aftermath: A Divided Championship

The Stecher Group, a loose alignment of Jack Curley, Paul Bowser, the Stechers and the Zbyszkos, struck first by scheduling a World Championship match between new champion Stanislaus Zbyszko and former champion Joe Stecher. It doesn't take a mind reader to know the purpose of the double-cross was to take the title from the Gold Dust Trio and put it back around Stecher's waist.

While Tom Packs, the St. Louis promoter, was rumored to be collaborating with conspirators, the Trio never knew for sure if Packs was involved. Packs did secure the title match though. Stecher and Zbyszko would meet on Saturday, May 30, 1925, in St. Louis at St. Louis University Field.

The Gold Dust Trio responded to the scheduling of the Zbyszko-Stecher match by scheduling a match between Lewis and

Munn for the same day. Lewis would wrestle Munn at the Floyd Fitzsimmons Blue Sky Arena in Michigan City, Michigan.

The story leading into this match was that when Munn dropped Lewis over the top rope, Lewis refused to recognize the legitimacy of his defeat.[ccxiii] Lewis refused to relinquish the title belt and took it with him on his tour of Europe.

Of course, it didn't square with the three months of promotion of Munn as World Champion, but the Gold Dust Trio were playing the hand they were dealt. All the confusion didn't hurt the gate for this match though.

15,000 fans crammed into the Blue-Sky Arena to see the Lewis-Munn match. Despite Munn's embarrassing loss a month earlier, Lewis allowed Munn to have a few moments in this match. In fact, Munn won the first fall from Lewis with the crotch hold and half-Nelson.[ccxiv]

In a touch thought up by Mondt, Munn refused to return to the ring until Lewis turned the title belt over to the referee. Lewis surrendered the belt setting up the remainder of the match.

As the second fall began, Lewis started to dominate. Lewis used twenty headlocks to secure the second fall in 17 minutes, 11 seconds. Seven more headlocks followed in the third fall. Lewis reclaimed a version of the world title by winning the third fall in 7 minutes.[ccxv]

Lewis stated he would soon meet the winner of the Zbyszko-Stecher match to reunify the title. Lewis learned quickly that Joe Stecher was not interested in soon.

Figure 43- Wayne "Big" Munn (Public Domain)

Wayne Munn would fade from the wrestling scene after this match. Formally retired from wrestling in 1926, Munn would move into the oil business. His wrestling career only lasted two years but it had a major impact on professional wrestling for the next 60 years.

The double-cross of Wayne Munn showed the danger of putting the championship on a pure performer, who could not protect himself, when a wrestler shot on him. Since promoters feared exposing the worked nature of professional wrestling, performers, no matter how popular, found it very difficult for promoters to book them to win a world title. Promoters would only forget the lesson of Wayne Munn when the performer drew such large crowds. If the performer could earn enough money, a promoter would take the risk but try to protect their champion.

History has viewed Munn as the goat in this story, but it is an unfair portrayal. Sandow recruited Munn into a big money position with promises to protect him. It is likely Munn saw his wrestling career as a chance to parlay his athletic ability into a good paying career.

The Gold Dust Trio in general, and Billy Sandow in particular, put him in this position. The Gold Dust Trio's business practices created lots of enemies.

Even Lewis must take his share of the blame for freezing Wladek Zbyszko and Joe Stecher out of the chance to wrestle him for the title. Lewis could beat both men in legitimate contests, so he wasn't worried about a double-cross. He simply wanted to cost them money by keeping them out of title matches.

Sandow was the most responsible though because he continued to ignore the warnings of Lewis and Mondt, who foresaw a double-cross. Had he listened to them, he could have avoided the situation entirely.

Tragically, on January 9, 1931, Munn died at Fort Sam Houston Hospital in San Antonio, Texas from the effects of Bright's disease. He had been gravely ill for 10 days prior to his death.[ccxvi] Munn was only 34 years old. Munn's wife Edna and daughter Mary Ann survived him.

On the same day as Lewis defeated Munn, Stanislaus Zbyszko, Munn's conqueror, wrestled Joe Stecher in front of 13,500 fans at St. Louis University Field. It was Joe Stecher's first title shot in four and half years. The 32-year-old Stecher had won his first world championship on July 5, 1915.

Stecher made Zbyszko look very good as he wrestled with him for 1 hour, 23 minutes before Stecher scored the first fall. Zbyszko appeared to fatigue, which allowed Stecher to secure the fall.[ccxvii]

Zbyszko's offense consisted of a couple of flying mares. Zbyszko spent much of the match fending off headlocks, arm bars and leg scissors. Stecher finally took the first fall with a body scissors.[ccxviii]

When Zbyszko returned to the ring, he lasted only 5 minutes before Stecher secured a second body scissors to secure the second fall. Stecher could now claim to be World Champion again.[ccxix] Stecher didn't make any statements about wrestling Lewis.

The quick second fall may have been an audible based on a legitimate injury. When Stecher took Zbyszko to the mat, he fell awkwardly on his chest and shoulder. As soon as the second fall was over, Wladek Zbyszko and another man helped Stanislaus to the back. Stanislaus Zbyszko immediately went to the hospital.[ccxx]

After an examination, the doctors discovered Zbyszko had a chest contusion and torn ligaments in his right shoulder. When promoters informed St. Louis Police of Zbyszko's injury, the police arrested Joe Stecher for assault with intent to kill. Stecher had to post $1,000 cash bond for the police to release him from jail.[ccxxi]

JOE STECHER.

Figure 44-The New World Champion from the May 31, 1925, St. Louis Post-Dispatch (Public Domain)

The police quickly dropped the charges, when Zbyszko made a statement exonerating Stecher. Zbyszko said he fell awkwardly, and the fall injured him more by accident than design.[ccxxii] Zbyszko recovered at his room in the Statler Hotel.

The gate for the Zbyszko-Stecher match was $43,315 plus Tom Packs received $15,000 for the film rights to the match.[ccxxiii] Unfortunately, the film company lost this footage over time.

According to the *St. Louis Post-Dispatch*, Tom Packs promised Zbyszko $40,000 plus Joe Stecher paid him $10,000 for the right to challenge for the title.[ccxxiv]

$40,000 from a $43,000 gate seems insane. If Packs received money from both Jack Curley and Paul Bowser to pay Zbyszko for the double-cross, it doesn't seem as ridiculous. If Zbyszko received $50,000 for the double-cross, it was a huge payoff. In 2021 dollars, it would be $763,000.

Stanislaus Zbyszko never told anyone why he double-crossed the Gold

Dust Trio, so we'll never know his exact motivation. Money would have been involved but long-term he may have earned more money with the Gold Dust Trio.

Once Zbyszko double-crossed the Gold Dust Trio, his career was effectively over. In a worked environment, once you execute a double-cross, you would often find yourself unable to find bookings. Even the promoters, you executed the double-cross for, would not trust you. If you double-crossed another promoter, you could double-cross them.

Did Zbyszko resent the Gold Dust Trio because he felt his world title reign should have been longer? Did he resent Lewis for freezing his beloved younger brother Wladek, who he lived with many times during his life even after both married, out of the world title contention? Did he know his career was winding down and wanted a big payday? It could have been all or none of these reasons. We will never really know.

Zbyszko did retire after dropping the title to Stecher. In 1928, he came out of retirement to wrestle the Great Gama. The Great Gama defeated him in 40 seconds. He made one more short-lived comeback in St. Louis with Tom Packs during 1937 but the almost 60-year-old only lasted a few months. Stanislaus Zbyszko's in-ring career was over after the double-cross.

In 1950, movie fans were reacquainted with Stanislaus Zbyszko in the movie *Night and the City* (1950). Despite being 70 years old, Zbyszko had one of the most credible wrestling scenes ever filmed with Mike Mazurki, another former professional wrestler. Still considered a classic, the film is well-worth a viewing.

Born on April 1, 1880, in Poland, Stanislaus Zbyszko passed away in St. Joseph, Missouri at the St. Joseph Hospital on September 22, 1967. Zbyszko had a heart attack 3 days earlier from which he never recovered. Zbyszko was 87 years old and lived on a nearby Savannah, Missouri farm with his brother Wladek and Wladek's wife. Zbyszko, a widower, was buried in Laurel Hills Cemetery in Saco, Maine with his deceased wife.

With the double-cross of Wayne Munn and the subsequent title switches, the world title was now divided. No one knew it at the time, but the situation would continue for 3 years before Lewis and Stecher could agree to a reunification match. Stecher and Lewis had to decide if it would be a work or a shoot?

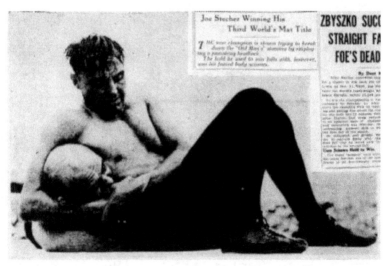

Figure 45-Stecher Wrestling Zbyszko at St. Louis University Field on May 30, 1925 (Public Domain)

Conclusion

Lewis and Stecher defended their versions of the world title quite differently. Lewis continued to defend his version of the world championship as if he were still the one and only legitimate World Heavyweight Wrestling Champion. Joe Stecher, fearing double-crosses, virtually retired the championship.

Stecher didn't completely trust his partners, a situation made worse by the subsequent actions of his partners. In March 1926, Stecher agreed to defend his title on a Paul Bowser card.

Bowser, the long-time Boston promoter, aroused Joe's, and Tony Stecher's suspicion by not telling them who he wanted Joe to wrestle. Tony, Joe's manager, demanded a $12,500 appearance guarantee.[ccxxv]

Bowser agreed but it didn't lessen their suspicion. Bowser's willingness to pay such a high fee further enflamed their concerns. Both brothers were on edge, when they arrived in Boston.

Initially, Jake Bressler entered the ring for the match. Both brothers visible relaxed as Bressler was not capable of defeating Stecher even if he surprised him with a double-cross.

Their peace was short-lived as known shooter Joe Malcewicz entered the ring in street clothes. Malcewicz challenged Stecher. He then stripped off his street clothes to reveal his wrestling attire underneath.[ccxxvi]

While Stecher was still probably a little better than Malcewicz, the match would not be a work but a contest with a dangerous wrestler. Stecher hadn't prepared for Malcewicz, who would be a significant challenge to his championship.

In response, Stecher did something that surprised Bowser. He simply left the ring. Bowser thought it was a ploy initially, but someone told him the Stecher brothers left the building.

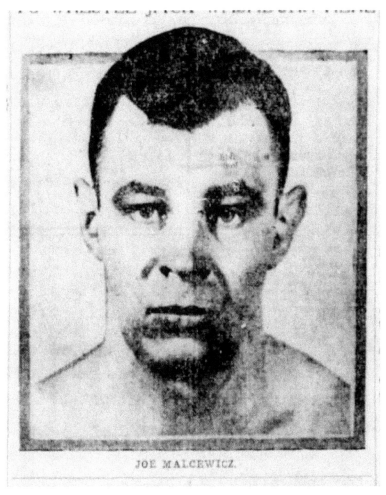

Figure 46- Joe Malcewicz (Public Domain)

When Bowser realized the Stechers were leaving town, he was stuck having to announce that the world champion would not be defending his title as advertised. This announcement nearly caused a riot and hurt Bowser's promotion for several months.[ccxxvii] The conspirators were finding it difficult to collaborate with each other.

If Bowser's actions put pressure on Stecher, the betrayal by a trusted friend later in 1926 cemented Stecher's belief that he couldn't trust anyone other than his brother.

As I stated earlier in the book, John "Tigerman" Pesek disliked the worked nature of professional wrestling. A skilled hooker, promoters were wary to putting Pesek in the ring with a champion other than Lewis for fear he would shoot on them and legitimately win the championship.

However, Pesek and Stecher had always been friendly. The two Nebraskans respected each other and worked matches many times. When Stecher won the title,

Pesek was one of the few men he booked to wrestle him.

Stecher and Pesek would wrestle three matches in 1926. The first two matches occurred with no issues. The matches were two-out-of-three-falls. Pesek would win a fall, but Stecher would win two falls to retain the title. Both matches drew large crowds leading to big paydays for both men.

They were looking forward to another nice payday going into their October 6, 1926, match in Los Angeles, California. The match followed a predictable pattern as the men split the first two falls. Entering the third fall, the men treated the fans to an exciting match.

As the men began the third fall, Pesek surprised Stecher by grabbing a wristlock and head scissors almost immediately.[ccxxviii] Stecher looked shocked as his old friend applied a legitimate submission hold.

Stecher quickly realized his predicament and tried to roll out of the hold but to no avail. Pesek was locked in. Stecher had no choice but to give up.[ccxxix]

As Stecher sat in the ring weeping, Pesek jumped around celebrating his apparent world title win. Pesek's joy was short-lived as the referee, who worked for the Stechers, disqualified Pesek for an "illegal hold" and awarded the third fall and match to Stecher.[ccxxx]

At first, the fans were quiet as they tried to process what was happening. Once they realized what had taken place, they began throwing seat cushions and bottles at the referee. The Los Angeles Police had to rush him from the ring before the berserk crowd killed him.[ccxxxi]

This match was disastrous for both men. Stecher retired the title and waited for his brother Tony to negotiate the eventual match with Ed Lewis to reunify the title.

Pesek found it impossible to find promoters to book him as no promoters trusted Pesek after he shot on Stecher.

Pesek ended up becoming one of the top greyhound dog trainers in the United States.

On Monday, February 20, 1928, the match between Lewis and Stecher finally took place. The match would be a legitimate contest between Lewis and Stecher to reunify the belt. Stecher's and Lewis' camps chose Tom Packs to promote the match, which would take place in the St. Louis Coliseum.

The double-cross and divided title had hurt wrestling across the country. Instead of the 15,000 fans who attended Lewis-Munn and the 13,500 fans who attended Stecher-Zbyszko on May 30, 1925, this match drew 7,000 fans. The fans, who did attend, watched a long, boring contest.

In Chapter 4 of *Hooker* by Lou Thesz, Lou Thesz states unequivocally that Lewis and Stecher were working with each other. However, Marcus Griffin in *Fall Guys* still claims the match was a shoot or contest. Both men had access to the same sources. Before I researched the match, I thought it was a work. After researching the match, they were both right.

The first fall seems like a legitimate contest between the old enemies. Lewis does not use a headlock at all in the match. The first fall also had long periods of inaction consistent with a contest. Neither man wanted to risk his opponent countering him.

For the first two hours of the match, Lewis pushed and shoved Stecher around the mat. Stecher's only offense was desperate dives at Lewis' leg to get a takedown.[ccxxxii]

After 2 hours, 16 minutes, Lewis secured a twisting arm lock on Stecher. Lewis twisted hard, forcing Stecher to turn to his back or have his shoulder separated. Lewis won the first fall at 2 hours, 16 minutes.[ccxxxiii]

Both men were legitimately exhausted as they returned to their dressing rooms. Instead of the normal 10-

minute intermission, the men stayed in the back for 20 minutes.[ccxxxiv] I believe Lewis and Stecher agreed to work the remainder of the match during this intermission.

When Lewis and Stecher returned to ring, Stecher scored his only real offense of the match. Stecher grabbed a wristlock and attempted to land his famous leg scissors. Lewis blocked the leg scissors, but Stecher held onto the wristlock. Lewis submitted to the wrist lock at the fifty-four second mark giving Stecher the second fall.[ccxxxv]

As they appeared before the battle: Lewis, at left; Harry Sharpe, referee and Joe Stecher.

Figure 47-Lewis and Stecher at mid-ring preparing for the match (Public Domain)

While they were working, Lewis remained careful in the third fall. Lewis slammed Stecher to mat twice before applying a wristlock. Lewis turned Stecher onto his back with the wristlock and the referee awarded the fall and match to Lewis in 12 minutes, 50 seconds.[ccxxxvi]

Stecher complained about the fall because his legs were clearly in the ropes. Normally, the referee would call for a break when a wrestler was touching the ropes.

However, Referee Sharp explained to the Athletic Commission that he told both men in pre-match instructions that unless the ropes were interfering with either man's offense or defense, he would not break the hold. The Missouri Athletic Commission upheld the referee's decision.[ccxxxvii] Ed "Strangler" Lewis was the unified World Heavyweight Wrestling Champion again.

The rope controversy was a Mondt invention to give Stecher an out, when the men decided to start working. Interestingly, Mondt swore to the day he died that this match was a shoot from start to finish.

One aspect of the match, which was a work, was the reported gate of $69,000 on an attendance of 7,000 people.[ccxxxviii] Tickets were normally $3 for the more expensive seats, so fans didn't pay $10 for tickets. If this amount included money both sides put up to make the match happen and film rights, it makes more sense.

Packs paid Stecher $29,000 for the match, while he paid Lewis $19,000.[ccxxxix] These figures are likely accurate because it would not have been cheap to end the divided title among enemy camps. The Gold Dust Trio desperately wanted to get Stecher in the ring, which explains his bigger percentage of the purse.

This match marked the end of an era in many ways. Many of the major players were entering the twilight of their careers.

Joe Stecher wrestled for a few more years but he was never world champion again. Stecher also experienced mental health issues during his last title reign.

When some con artists on the road took advantage of him in the early 1930s, the resulting financial loss further aggravated his mental health challenges.[ccxl] Stecher never recovered from the con men bilking him out of his savings. His brother Tony put him in a series of mental health facilities. Joe Stecher remained in institutions until his death at 80 years of age in 1974.

Lou Thesz stated when he first wrestled for Tony Stecher, who was promoting wrestling in Minneapolis, Minnesota, he got to meet Joe Stecher. This meeting occurred in late 1935 or early 1936, when Stecher was 42 years old.[ccxli]

Stecher had not wrestled or trained for 4 or 5 years by this time but easily defeated Thesz and four other wrestlers.

Thesz said Stecher was never winded. He never forgot his encounter with the legendary champion.[ccxlii]

The match also spelt the end of the Gold Dust Trio. Tension had been growing between Sandow and Mondt since the double-cross. Mondt would have left earlier but he was working out with Lewis in preparation for the Stecher match.

Once Lewis regained the title, Mondt left the promotion. Lewis remained loyal to Sandow and stayed but his career was also winding down. Lewis, who would turn 40 in 1931, was already losing his eyesight due to trachoma.

Bacteria spread trachoma. It causes hardening of the inner eyelid in the early stages, followed by actual eye damage and blindness in the later stages. The disease is treatable with antibiotics today but at the time of Lewis' infection, there was no cure. Lewis caught the dreaded disease off dirty wrestling mats.

By the time of the Stecher match, Lewis saw most people as outlines. Sandow had to lead Lewis to the ring by the arm for the Stecher match.[ccxliii]

In the early 1930s, Lewis and Sandow had a falling out, when John Pesek thought he should win a match in Kansas City over Lewis, who returned from a European trip in terrible shape. An enraged Lewis told Pesek, "We are wrestling tonight."[ccxliv]

Sandow tried to talk Lewis into working with Pesek because he feared Pesek may beat Lewis in his weakened condition. Lewis refused to cooperate. Sandow, who had a terrible temper, slammed the door, and left. It was the end of their partnership. Lewis beat Pesek in two straight falls despite his poor physical condition.[ccxlv]

Sandow was never a big force in professional wrestling after the break-up of the Gold Dust Trio. Lewis wrestled sporadically. He did win a few more world titles, after the current champions made him mad, even though he was almost blind. Lewis primarily put over future champions like Jim Londos. Lewis also taught future wrestling legends Lou Thesz and "Judo" Gene LeBell. Lewis would be Thesz' manager and advisor during Thesz's National Wrestling Alliance world title reign.

Figure 48-"Toots" Mondt, on the right, applying a hold in 1924 (Public Domain)

Unlike his former partners, Joseph "Toots" Mondt had the longest career in professional wrestling. He was starting his promotional and booking career prior to the Stecher-Lewis match. Between 1928 and 1969, he twice ran a booking office in New York and once ran a booking office in Los Angeles. Mondt also assisted with the promotions in those cities.

Mondt was critical to the development of the World Wide Wrestling Federation (WWWF) under Vincent J. McMahon in the early 1960s. Mondt's business practices led to a mixed reputation though.

In the 1930s, the New York Athletic Commission suspended Mondt for attempting to bribe officials in an attempted double-cross of World Heavyweight Wrestling Champion Jim Londos.[ccxlvi] Mondt was involved with the successful double-cross of Londos, when Londos wrestled Joe Savoldi in 1933.

In 1938, the widow of wrestler Mike Romano sued Mondt.[ccxlvii] Mrs. Romano said her husband loaned Mondt a championship wrestling belt, worth an approximate $2,000, to push one of his wrestlers, Dave Levin.

Mondt, in a letter to her lawyer, stated Mr. Romano gave him the belt. She quoted him as saying, "The belt is constructed of webbing interspersed with some sapphire stones and small diamond chips which wouldn't run into a whole lot of money."[ccxlviii] Mondt moved from New York to California in the late 1930s because of the heat his machinations were bringing on his New York partners.

Unlike his promotional mentor Billy Sandow, Mondt was a poor payoff man. Most of his wrestlers thought he was holding back some of their money to support his reported gambling habit. Lou Thesz considered Mondt a thief and openly detested him.[ccxlix]

Mondt may not have enjoyed such a long career except for his ability to book wrestlers, wrestling angles and deliver a crowd-pleasing style of wrestling. Even detractors, like Lou Thesz, admitted few, if anyone, understood the art of professional wrestling as well as "Toots" Mondt. Bruno Sammartino called him a genius.

In 1969, 75-year-old Mondt finally retired. He sold his shares in the WWWF promotion and moved back to his wife Alda's hometown of St. Louis, Missouri. They initially moved back to care for his mother-in-law. After she died two years later, they decided to stay. Mondt would often have lunch with his old friend, and long-time St. Louis promoter, Sam Muchnick.[ccl] Mondt died in 1976 and is buried in St. Louis' Calvary Cemetery.

Mondt and his partners ruled wrestling during one of its golden eras. From 1923 to 1925, the Gold Dust Trio could boast of a license to print money. Ed "Strangler" Lewis earned more money from box office gates than any other athlete of the decade. The Gold Dust Trio kept their wrestlers happy with regular, generous payoffs. The new, faster paced wrestling drew many more fans to the matches.

Like so many other combinations, greed and ambition would spell the end of the Gold Dust Trio. However, their legend endures in the sporting exhibition they helped change and popularize. The Gold Dust Trio holds a place with the National Wrestling Alliance in the 1940s and 1950s, as well as the WWF in the 1980s, as a group that changed professional wrestling in historical ways. For five years, they were the kings of the sport.

Figure 49-Ed "Strangler" Lewis in 1924 (Public Domain)

Other Combat Sports Books by Ken Zimmerman Jr.

Masked Marvel To The Rescue: The Gimmick That Saved the 1915 New York Wrestling Tournament

Gotch vs. Hackenschmidt: The Matches That Made and Destroyed Legitimate American Professional Wrestling

Evan "The Strangler" Lewis: The Most Feared Wrestler of the 19th Century

William Muldoon: The Solid Man Conquers Wrestling and Physical Culture

Morrissey vs. Poole: Politics, Prizefighting and the Murder of Bill the Butcher

Bibliography

Newspapers

Alaska Daily Empire (Juneau, Alaska)

Arizona Republican (Phoenix, Arizona)

Beatrice Daily Sun (Beatrice, Nebraska)

Birmingham News (Birmingham, Alabama)

Bridgeport Times and Evening Farmer
(Bridgeport, Connecticut)

Capital Journal (Salem, Oregon)

Evening Capital News (Boise, Idaho)

Evening Journal (Wilmington, Delaware)

Evening Star (Washington D.C.)

Grand Island Daily Independent (Grand
Island, Nebraska)

Great Falls Tribune (Great Falls,
Montana)

Indiana Daily Times (Indianapolis,

Indiana)

Indiana Gazette (Indiana, Pennsylvania)

The Indianapolis Times

Lakeland Evening Telegram (Lakeland,
Florida)

The Kansas City Star (Kansas City,
Missouri)

New York Evening World

New York Herald

New York Tribune

Omaha Daily Bee

Omaha Morning Bee

Ogden Standard-Examiner

Perth Amboy Evening News (Perth Amboy,
Pennsylvania)

Philadelphia Inquirer

Pittsburgh Post-Gazette

Pueblo Chieftain

Richmond Palladium and Sun-Telegram

(Richmond, Virginia)

Richmond Planet

Rock Island Argus and Daily Times (Rock Island, IL)

Seattle Star

South Bend News-Times

St. Louis Post-Dispatch

St. Louis Star and Times

Tampa Times (Tampa, Florida)

The Wheeling Intelligencer (Wheeling, W. VA)

Times Union (Brooklyn, NY)

Topeka State Journal

Washington Herald

Washington Times

Books

Fall Guys by Marcus Griffin

Hooker by Lou Thesz

Websites

www.wrestlingdata.com

www.newspapers.com

legacyofwrestling.com

About the Author

Ken Zimmerman Jr. is a married father and grandfather, who lives outside of St. Louis, Missouri. Ken has been interested in combat sports since watching professional wrestling from St. Louis in the late 1970s. His stepdad, Ernest Charles Diaz, introduced him to boxing in 1981. A lifelong martial artist, Ken holds rank in three martial arts including a 4th Degree black belt in Taekwondo.

If you like this book, you can sign up for Ken's newsletter to receive information about future book releases. You can sign up for the newsletter and receive bonus e-books by going to www.kenzimmermanjr.com and signing up for the newsletter.

Endnotes

Introduction
[i] Legacyofwrestling.com, History of the Wichita Wrestling Territory
[ii] Wrestlingdata.com
[iii] Hooker by Lou Thesz, Chapter 4
[iv] Ibid

Chapter 1
[v] Hooker by Lou Thesz, Chapter 1
[vi] New York Tribune, December 14, 1920, p. 17
[vii] Ibid
[viii] Ibid
[ix] Ibid
[x] Ibid. When I attended matches in St. Louis, Missouri with my older sister Vicky in 1981 and 1982, the Kiel Auditorium would fill up with smoke after the first couple matches. The wrestlers would wrestle in a fog.
[xi] Ibid
[xii] Ibid
[xiii] Ibid
[xiv] Ibid
[xv] Ibid. The head scissors are one of the Brazilian Jiu-Jitsu escapes to the headlock. In actual competitions, this hold would be a viable counter to a headlock.
[xvi] Ibid
[xvii] Hooker by Lou Thesz, Chapter 4

Chapter 2
[xviii] Ogden Standard-Examiner, January 7, 1921, p. 13
[xix] New York Herald, January 15, 1921, p. 12
[xx] Ibid
[xxi] Washington Times, January 15, 1921, p. 15
[xxii] Pueblo Chieftain, January 7, 1921, p. 6
[xxiii] Washington Herald, January 16, 1921, p. 7
[xxiv] New York Herald, January 22, 1921, p. 10
[xxv] New York Tribune, January 22, 1921, p. 11
[xxvi] New York Tribune, January 25, 1921, p. 13

[xxvii] New York Herald, January 25, 1921, p. 13 (The coverage between the New York Tribune and New York Herald varied including the weight of each contestant.)
[xxviii] Ibid
[xxix] New York Tribune, January 25, 1921, p. 13
[xxx] New York Herald, January 25, 1921, p. 13
[xxxi] Ibid
[xxxii] Ibid
[xxxiii] Ibid
[xxxiv] New York Evening World, January 27, 1921, p. 18
[xxxv] St. Louis Post-Dispatch, August 25, 1950, p. 18
[xxxvi] Evening Star, July 18, 1950, p. A18
[xxxvii] Evening Star, August 26, 1950, p. B9
[xxxviii] Great Falls Tribune, January 28, 1921, p. 6
[xxxix] Ibid
[xl] New York Tribune, February 1, 1921, p. 10
[xli] Washington Times, February 3, 1921, p. 18
[xlii] Arizona Republican, February 18, 1921, p. 1
[xliii] Ogden Standard-Examiner, February 24, 1921, Last Edition, p. 2
[xliv] P. 16

Chapter 3

[xlv] Evening Capital News (Boise, Idaho), January 4, 1920, p. 9
[xlvi] Bridgeport Times and Evening Farmer, February 13, 1920, p. 14
[xlvii] New York Tribune, February 29, 1920, p. 18
[xlviii] Omaha Daily Bee, June 13, 1920, p. 19
[xlix] Topeka State Journal, January 17, 1921, p. 3
[l] Omaha Daily Bee, January 30, 1921, p. 15. Newspapers frequently misspelled names in the 19th and 20th Centuries. Wrestlers from foreign countries were particularly the victims of these misspellings.
[li] Indiana Daily Times, February 9, 1921, p. 8
[lii] Evening Star (Washington, D.C.), February 11, 1921, p. 24
[liii] New York Tribune, February 11, 1921, p. 11
[liv] Arizona Republic, February 18, 1921, p. 2
[lv] Ibid
[lvi] New York Tribune, March 4, 1921, p. 12
[lvii] New York Tribune, March 8, 1921, p. 13
[lviii] New York Tribune, March 15, 1921, p. 13
[lix] Evening Star (Washington, D.C.), March 15, 1921, p. 27
[lx] New York Herald, March 15, 1921, p. 14

Chapter 4

[lxi] Evening Star (Washington, D.C.), April 14, 1921, p. 31

[lxii] Omaha Daily Bee, April 24, 1921, p. 18

[lxiii] Omaha Daily Bee, May 3, 1921, p. 8

[lxiv] Ibid

[lxv] New York Tribune, May 7, 1921, p. 12

[lxvi] Ibid

[lxvii] Ibid

[lxviii] Ibid

[lxix] South Bend News-Time, May 7, 1921, Morning Edition, p. 11

[lxx] Times Union (Brooklyn, New York), May 7, 1921, p. 8

[lxxi] San Francisco Examiner, May 2, 1917, p. 15

Chapter 5

[lxxii] Evening Journal (Wilmington, Delaware), May 24, 1921, p. 14

[lxxiii] Ibid

[lxxiv] Arizona Republican, May 27, 1921, p. 1

[lxxv] Arizona Republican, May 28, 1921, p. 1

[lxxvi] The Wheeling Intelligencer, May 31, 1921, p. 8

[lxxvii] Birmingham News, June 4, 1921, p. 8

[lxxviii] Omaha Daily Bee, June 12, 1921, p.5

[lxxix] Rock Island Argus and Daily Union, June 23, 1921, p. 12

[lxxx] Ibid

[lxxxi] Richmond Palladium and Sun-Telegram, July 23, 1921, p. 9

[lxxxii] Ibid

[lxxxiii] Great Falls Tribune, November 8, 1921, p. 8

[lxxxiv] Ibid

[lxxxv] Great Falls Tribune, November 13, 1921, p. 12

[lxxxvi] Great Falls Tribune, November 21, 1921, p. 12

[lxxxvii] New York Tribune, November 29, 1921, p. 13

[lxxxviii] Ibid

[lxxxix] Ibid

[xc] Ibid

[xci] Ibid

Chapter 6

[xcii] South Bend News-Times, December 12, 1921, Morning Edition, p. 7

[xciii] Ibid

[xciv] Ibid

[xcv] Ibid

[xcvi] Evening Star. December 16, 1921, p. 30
[xcvii] Ibid
[xcviii] Ibid
[xcix] Bridgeport Times and Evening Farmer, February 7, 1922, p. 4
[c] Wrestlingdata.com, Earl Caddock profile
[ci] New York Herald, February 7, 1922, p. 12
[cii] Ibid
[ciii] Ibid
[civ] Ibid
[cv] Ibid
[cvi] Ibid
[cvii] Ibid
[cviii] Omaha Daily Bee, February 7, 1922, p. 8
[cix] Ibid
[cx] Ibid
[cxi] Omaha Daily Bee, January 8, 1922, p. 15
[cxii] Ogden Standard Examiner, February 22, 1922, p. 2
[cxiii] Ibid

Chapter 7

[cxiv] Capital Journal, March 4, 1922, p. 5
[cxv] Pueblo Chieftain, March 4, 1922, p. 14
[cxvi] Capital Journal, March 4, 1922, p. 5
[cxvii] Ibid
[cxviii] Lakeland Evening Telegram, March 4, 1922, p. 6
[cxix] Indiana Daily Times, March 8, 1922, p. 10
[cxx] Ibid
[cxxi] Ibid
[cxxii] Ibid
[cxxiii] Bridgeport Times and Evening Farmer, March 13, 1922, p. 8
[cxxiv] Capital Journal (Salem, Oregon), March 16, 1922, p. 8
[cxxv] Ibid
[cxxvi] Topeka State Journal, March 25, 1922, p. 6
[cxxvii] Ibid
[cxxviii] Ogden Standard-Examiner, April 14, 1922, p. 14
[cxxix] Ibid
[cxxx] Beatrice Daily Sun (Beatrice, Nebraska), April 26, 1922, p. 6
[cxxxi] Lake County Times (Hammond, Indiana) April 26, 1922, p. 10
[cxxxii] Omaha Daily Bee, May 25, 1922, p. 12
[cxxxiii] Morning Tulsa Daily World, July 4, 1922, p. 9
[cxxxiv] Ibid

[cxxxv] Ibid

[cxxxvi] St. Louis Star-Times, December 11, 1922, p. 16

[cxxxvii] St. Louis Star-Times, December 15, 1922, p. 20

[cxxxviii] Ibid

[cxxxix] Ibid

[cxl] Ibid

[cxli] Ibid

[cxlii] Ibid

[cxliii] Ibid

[cxliv] Ibid

[cxlv] Ibid

[cxlvi] The Pensacola Journal, December 27, 1922, p. 2

Chapter 8

[cxlvii] I covered this story extensively in one of my previous books Gotch vs. Hackenschmidt (2016).

[cxlviii] Ogden Standard-Examiner, April 26, 1922, p. 10

[cxlix] Ibid

[cl] Ogden Standard-Examiner, May 10, 1922, p. 10

[cli] The Evening Herald (Albuquerque, New Mexico), May 31, 1922, p. 4

[clii] Ibid

[cliii] Evening Star (Washington, DC), November 11, 1922, p. 8

[cliv] Ogden Standard-Examiner, November 14, 1922, p. 11

[clv] Ibid

[clvi] Fall Guys: The Barnums of Bounce by Marcus Griffin, Chapter 4

Chapter 9

[clvii] Hooker by Lou Thesz

[clviii] Fall Guys, Chapter 4

[clix] I wrote extensively about these tournaments in Masked Marvel to the Rescue (2020), which covers both tournaments and the gimmick needed to save the Fall Tournament.

[clx] Fall Guys, Chapter 5

[clxi] Fall Guys, Chapter 5

Chapter 10

[clxii] Omaha Daily Bee, January 13, 1923, p. 11

[clxiii] Ibid

[clxiv] Perth Amboy Evening News, February 16, 1923, p. 23

[clxv] Kansas City Star, May 3, 1923, p. 12

clxvi Ibid
clxvii St. Louis Star and Times, October 7, 1926, p. 16
clxviii The Indianapolis Times, March 26, 1923, p. 7
clxix Ibid
clxx Fall Guys, Chapter 8
clxxi Hooker by Lou Thesz
clxxii Evening Star (Washington, D.C.), May 23, 1923, p. 28
clxxiii Omaha Morning Bee, December 14, 1923, p. 9
clxxiv Alaska Daily Empire, October 19, 1923, p. 5
clxxv Brownsville Herald (Brownsville, Texas), January 2, 1924, p. 5
clxxvi St. Louis Star and Times, February 27, 1924, p. 15
clxxvii Ibid
clxxviii Ibid
clxxix Omaha Morning Bee, May 7, 1924, p. 10
clxxx Ibid
clxxxi The Alaska Daily Empire, August 12, 1924, p. 5
clxxxii Ibid
clxxxiii Richmond Planet, August 23, 1924, p. 7

Chapter 11
clxxxiv Omaha Morning Bee, March 5, 1924, p. 8
clxxxv Omaha Daily Bee, March 27, 1924, p. 11
clxxxvi Omaha Morning Bee, May 13, 1924, p. 6
clxxxvii Omaha Morning Bee, June 5, 1924, p.10
clxxxviii Seattle Star, August 4, 1924, p. 11
clxxxix The Kansas City Times, October 25, 1924, p. 10
cxc Ibid
cxci The Kansas City Times, November 20, 1924, p. 14
cxcii Ibid
cxciii The Kansas City Star, December 12, 1924, p. 24
cxciv Kansas City Star, January 9, 1925, p. 16
cxcv Ibid
cxcvi Ibid
cxcvii Ibid
cxcviii Ibid
cxcix Ibid

Chapter 12
No Endnotes

Chapter 13

[cc] Kansas City Times, February 12, 1925, p. 14
[cci] Ibid
[ccll] Ibid
[cciii] Ibid
[cciv] Ibid
[ccv] The Indiana Gazette (Indiana, Pennsylvania), March 7, 1925, p. 5
[ccvi] The Philadelphia Inquirer, April 16, 1925, p. 23
[ccvii] Ibid
[ccviii] Ibid
[ccix] Ibid
[ccx] Ibid
[ccxi] Ibid
[ccxii] Ibid

Chapter 14

[ccxiii]St. Louis Post-Dispatch, May 31, 1925, p. 12
[ccxiv] Ibid
[ccxv] Ibid
[ccxvi] Grand Island Daily Independent (Grand Island, Nebraska), January 9, 1931, p. 7
[ccxvii] St. Louis Post-Dispatch, May 31, 1925, p. 9
[ccxviii] Ibid
[ccxix] Ibid
[ccxx] Ibid
[ccxxi] St. Louis Post-Dispatch, May 31, 1925, p. 1
[ccxxii] Ibid
[ccxxiii] St. Louis Post-Dispatch, May 31, 1925, p. 10
[ccxxiv] Ibid

Conclusion

[ccxxv] Tampa Times, March 12, 1926, p. 35
[ccxxvi] Ibid
[ccxxvii] Ibid
[ccxxviii] St. Louis Star and Times, October 7, 1926, p. 16
[ccxxix] Ibid
[ccxxx] Ibid
[ccxxxi] Ibid
[ccxxxii] St. Louis Post-Dispatch, February 21, 1928, p. 24-25
[ccxxxiii] Ibid

[ccxxxiv] Ibid

[ccxxxv] Ibid

[ccxxxvi] Ibid

[ccxxxvii] Ibid

[ccxxxviii] St. Louis Post-Dispatch, February 21, 1928, p. 25

[ccxxxix] Ibid

[ccxl] Hooker by Lou Thesz, Chapter 3

[ccxli] Ibid

[ccxlii] Ibid

[ccxliii] Fall Guys by Marcus Griffin

[ccxliv] Hooker, Chapter 4

[ccxlv] Ibid

[ccxlvi] St. Louis Star and Times, April 12, 1933, p. 19

[ccxlvii] St. Louis Star and Times, October 13, 1938, p. 32

[ccxlviii] Ibid

[ccxlix] Hooker, Chapter 4

[ccl] St. Louis Post-Dispatch, February 1, 1976, p. 38

CPSIA information can be obtained
at www.ICGtesting.com
Printed in the USA
LVHW010004071222
734695LV00004B/379

9 781087 857343